MOUNTAIN BIKE TRAILS

of

Wisconsin

Illustrated Maps by

American Bike Trails

MOUNTAIN BIKE TRAILS
of Wisconsin

Designed for easy reference by all biker levels

Published by   American Bike Trails
1430 Miner St., Suite 525
Des Plaines, IL 60016

Created by   Ray Hoven
Design by   Mary C. Rumpsa

Contents

How to use this book 01

Terms used 02

Riding tips 03

Wisconsin Map 05

Section 1   *South East Wisconsin* 06

     Bong State Recreation Trail 08

     Devil's Lake State Park 10

     Harrington Beach State Park 12

     Kohler-Andrae State Park 13

     Kettle Moraine State Forest - North Unit 14

       Greenbush Recreation Area/Zillmer Trails 16

       New Fane Trails 17

     Kettle Moraine State Forest - South Unit 18

       John Muir Trails 20

       Emma F. Carlin Trails/Eagle-McMiller Areas 22

     Lapham Peak 23

Section 2   *South West Wisconsin* 24

     Blue Mound State Park 26

     Wildcat Mountain State Park 27

     Governor Dodge State Park 28

     Mirror Lake State Park 30

     Perrot State Park 31

     Wyalusing State Park 32

Section 3   *North East Wisconsin* 34

     High Cliff State Park 36

     Oconto County Recreational Trail 38

     Newport State Park 40

     Door County 41

     Peninsula State Park 42

     Potawatomi State Park 44

     Point Beach State Forest 46

Section 4   *West Central Wisconsin* 48

     Black River State Forest 50

       Castle Mound Park 52

       Pigeon Creek 53

       Smrekar & Wildcat 54

     Lake Wissota State Park 56

     Lowes Creek County Park 58

Contents (continued)

Section 5   *North Central Wisconsin* 60
Council Grounds State Park 62
The Hiawatha Trail 64
Lumberjack Trail 66
Madeline Lake Trails 68
McNaughton Lake Trails 69
Nine Mile County Forest Trail 70
Shannon Lake Trail 72
Chequamegon National Forest - Taylor County 73
Jaycee Trail, Timm's Hill Trail 74

Section 6   *North West Wisconsin* 76
Black Lake Trail 78
Governor Knowles State Forest 79
Brule River State Forest 80
Copper Falls State Park 82
Flambeau River State Forest 84
Tuscobia-Park Falls State Trail 86
Rock Lake 88
Wintergreen 89

Section 7   *North West Wisconsin - CAMBA Clusters* 92
Delta Cluster 94
Drummond Cluster 96
Cable Cluster 98
Seeley Cluster 100
HaywardCluster 102
Namakagon Cluster 104

Canoeing in Wisconsin 106

Wisconsin Tourism Information 108

Available Detail Trail Maps 112

Order Form 120

Index 124

How to Use this Book

You will find this book a comprehensive, easy-to-use, quick-reference to many of the Mountain Biking Trails in Wisconsin. The book contains over 50 detailed trail maps, plus maps covering state sectionals and forest areas.

The book is organized by geographic section. Each section consists of a trail index and graphical overview followed by illustrated maps and specific information for each trail. In addition, such helpful features as location and access, trail facilities, distance and populations of nearby communities are included.

FACILITIES

- 🛠 **Bicycle Service**
- Ⓐ **Camping**
- **Canoe Launch**
- ➕ **First Aid**
- ❓ **Information/Park Office**
- **Lodging**
- Ⓟ **Parking**
- **Picnic Area**
- **Refreshments**
- **Restrooms**
- **Shelter**
- **Water**
- **MF** **Multi-Facilities Available**
  First Aid   Lodging
  Picnic   Refreshments
  Restrooms   Telephone

TRAIL TYPES

- —— **Mountain Biking trail**
- ▪▪▪ **Leisure Biking trail**
- ══ **Cross-Country Skiing**
- ⋯⋯ **Snowmobile trail**
- === **Hiking Trail**
- ▬ ▬ **Horseback Riding Trail**

TRAIL USES

- 🚴 **Mountain biking**
- 🚴 **Leisure biking**
- **Cross-Country Skiing**
- **Snowmobiling**
- **Hiking**
- **Horseback riding**

AREA DESCRIPTION

- **Park**
- **Waterway**
- **Marsh**
- **Mile scale**
- **Directional**

ROADS

- —— **Street**
- 45 **Interstate Highway**
- 45 **U.S. Highway**
- 45 **State Highway**
- JJ **County Highway**

Terms Used

Length		Expressed in miles. Round trip mileage is normally indicated for loops.
Effort Level	*Easy*	Physical exertion is not strenuous. Climbs and descents as well as technical obstacles are more minimal. Recommended for beginners.
	Moderate	Physical exertion is not excessive. Climbs and descents can be challenging. Expect some technical obstacles.
	Difficult	Physical exertion is demanding. Climbs and descents require good riding skills. Trail surface may be sandy, loose rock, soft or wet.
Directions		Describes by way of directions and distances, how to get to the trail areas from roads and nearby communities.
Map		Illustrative representation of a geographic area, such as a state, section, forest, park or trail complex.
Forest		Typically encompasses a dense growth of trees and underbrush covering a large tract.
Park		A tract of land generally including woodlands and open areas.
DNR		Department of Natural Resources

Types of Biking

Mountain	Fat-tired bikes are recommended. Ride may be generally flat but then with a soft, rocky or wet surface.
Leisure	Off-road gentle ride. Surface is generally paved or screened.
Tour	Riding on roads with motorized traffic or on road shoulders.

Riding Tips

- In Wisconsin, the wind is usually out of the southwest. Consider riding west in the early morning when the wind is calm, and then east in the afternoon with the wind at your back.

- Pushing in gears that are too high can push knees beyond their limits. Avoid extremes by pedaling faster rather than shifting into a higher gear.

- Keeping your elbows bent, changing your hand position frequently and wearing bicycle gloves all help to reduce the numbness or pain in the palm of the hand from long-distance riding.

- Keep you pedal rpms up on an uphill so you have reserve power if you lose speed.

- Stay in a high-gear on a level surface, placing pressure on the pedals and resting on the handle bars and saddle.

- Lower your center of gravity on a long or steep downhill run by using the quick release seat post binder and dropping the saddle height down.

- Rocking the bike gives you more efficient pumping. This means pulling up on the left hand grip as you push down the left pedal and vice versa.

- Brake intermittently on a rough surface.

- Complete your braking process before bumping over sizable objects.

- If your wheel drops into a deep rut, brake to a stop immediately. If you try to climb out, the front wheel will jam.

- When riding over thick sticks or branches, make sure to cross them close to their mid-sections. Hitting one near its end can flip it up into your spokes.

- Never start biking on unfamiliar trails late in the day and always carry a compass.

- Cross-country trail systems used for biking are commonly marked in kilometers, which is roughly two thirds of a mile.

Riding Tips (continued)

- Expect to average less than 5 miles per hour on extremely rough trails, 5 to 10 miles per hour on moderate terrain and 10 to 14 miles per hour on gravel or paved surfaces.

- Be sensitive to the trail surface to insure little damage is done.

- Hikers have the right-of-way. Moderate your speed and communicate so that hikers are aware of your presence.

- Make advance reservations for lodging and camping wherever possible. Campers arriving by bicycle are now accommodated at state parks in special areas,without advance reservations.

Clothing

Dress warmly in cool weather. Keep your head, chest and knees warm. Bike shorts or seamless apparel is recommended. Leg clothing should be worn when the temperature is below 65 degrees. Shoes should have firm soles. Use padded gloves.

Don't Forget

Map	Water
First Aid Kit	Pocket Knife
Pocket Money	Pack Jacket
High Energy Foods	Rack Strap

Note:
Most trails are generally open to hiking

State of Wisconsin

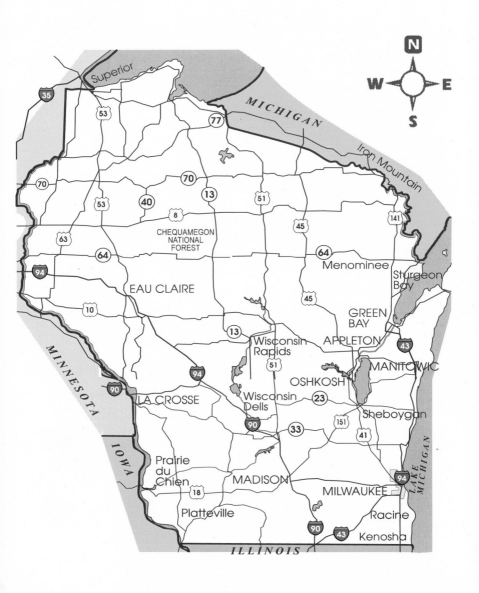

SOUTH EAST
Mountain Biking Trails

section
1

Bong State Recreation Trail 8

Devil's Lake State Park 10

Harrington Beach State Park 12

Kohler-Andrae State Park 13

Kettle Moraine State Forest - North Unit 14

    Greenbush Recreation Area 16

    Zillmer Trails 16

    New Fane Trails 17

Kettle Moraine State Forest - South Unit 18

    John Muir Trails 20

    Emma F. Carlin Trails 22

    Eagle/McMiller/Old World Wisconsin Areas 22

Lapham Peak 23

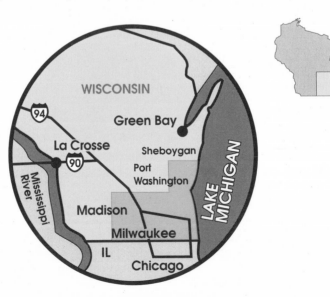

American BikeTrails

EMERGENCY ASSISTANCE

Your first contact in an emergency should be the park office. If no one is available, dial 911, giving detail and your location within the park.

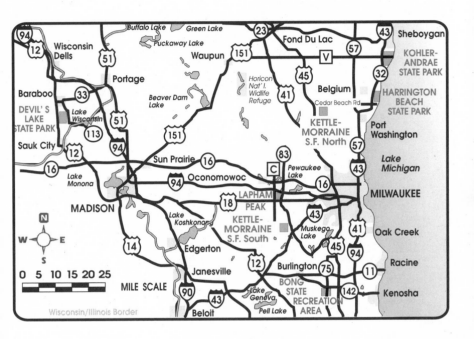

WISCONSIN STATE PARKS

Day use is from 6 a.m. to 11 p.m.

Vehicle parking stickers are required, and are available at park offices.

Trail passes are required for bikers 16 years and older.

Passes are daily or annual and are good on all Wisconsin State Trails.

Hikers have the right of way.

Park roads are generally open to bicycle use.

Designated Areas - those areas which are inspected and maintained by park staff. You are encouraged to limit your activities to designated areas.

Area Overview

Bong State Recreation Area

Trail Length	12.0 miles
Effort Level	Easy
Setting	Level to rolling terrain. Prairie, woodlands, wetlands.
Location	From Kenosha, 16 miles west on Hwy 142 to entrance. From Burlington, 8 miles southeast on Hwy 142.
Information	Bong Park Office 26313 Burlington Road, Kansasville, WI 53139 (414) 652-0377 (414) 878-5600

North Loops
Gray	**1.7 miles**	**(2.7 km)**

Gentle terrain through prairie with scattered woodlands.

Orange **6.4 miles** **(10.3 km)**
Level to rolling terrain. Pit Toilet, hand pump, picnic tables located at the trail's north end, off Hwy. BB.

Red **8.3 miles** **(13.4 km)**
Gentle with no steep grades.

Yellow **4.4 miles** **(7.1 km)**
Level to moderately rolling crossing prairies, wetlands and woodlands. There is one steep hill with a stairway that provides an excellent view of northwest Bong.

South Loops

Green **1.8 miles** **(2.9 km)**
Gentle terrain through rolling prairies, scattered woodlands and ponds. Nice East Lake view.

Blue **4.2 miles** **(6.8 km)**
Gentle to moderate terrain with steep hills, passing East Lake Beach where you will find restrooms and water.

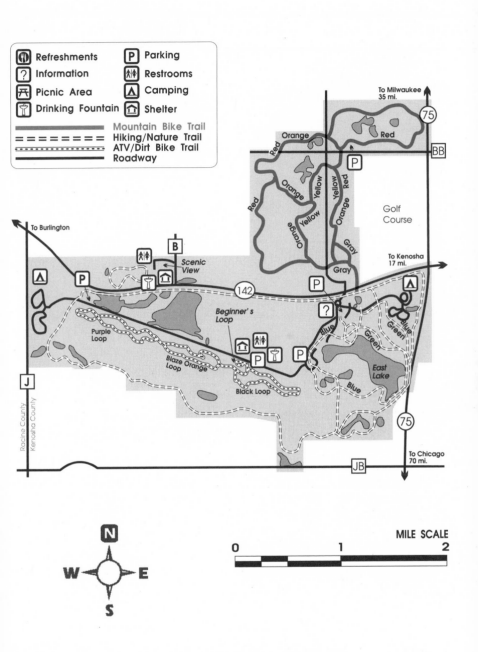

Bong State Recreation Area

Devil's Lake State Park

Trail Length   6.5 miles Bicycles are only allowed on the Ice Age Loop and a connector trail. Most trails are color coded.

Effort Level   Easy to Difficult—Metal squares attached to posts or trees.

Setting   A generally medium effort trail that is long, winding and grassy with variable grades through fields, bushy areas and woods. Scenic views from the top of the East Bluff on the south end.

Location   3 miles south of Baraboo on Hwy. 123

Information   Devil's Lake State Park
S5975 Park Road
Baraboo, WI 53913
(608) 356-8301

Comments   Although Devil's Lake State Park is the most popular park in Wisconsin, there are times during the biking season when the park is not crowded. Take time to visit Baraboo, the home-town of the Ringling Brothers, and the Circus World Museum. It is a living museum with beautifully restored hand-carved circus wagons, clowns, animals and daring performers.

Ice Age Loop 🚲   (Red) 4.0 miles

A generally medium effort trail that is long, winding and grassy with variable grades through fields, bushy areas and woods. Scenic views from the top of the East Bluff on the south end.

Hiking Trails 🚶

Balanced Rock   .3 miles
Difficult, steep climbing with stone steps. Great views of Devil's Lake and the Balanced Rock formation.
CCC Trail   (Purple)   .6 miles
Difficult, steep climbing with stone steps. Many scenic views.
Devil's Doorway   (Purple)   .5 miles
Easy, level asphalt trail along top edge of East Bluff. There is a side trail with stone steps leading you to the Devil's Doorway rock formation.
East Bluff Trail   (Orange)   1.3 miles
Medium effort, asphalt with stone steps. Winds back and forth between the edge of the bluff and the adjacent woods. Goes to top of East Bluff. Elephant Cave and Elephant Rock are at the north end.
East Bluff Woods   (Yellow)   1.3 miles
Easy to medium. Gravel and grassy in woods with a steep grade on the East Bluff between the North Shore and Balanced Rock.

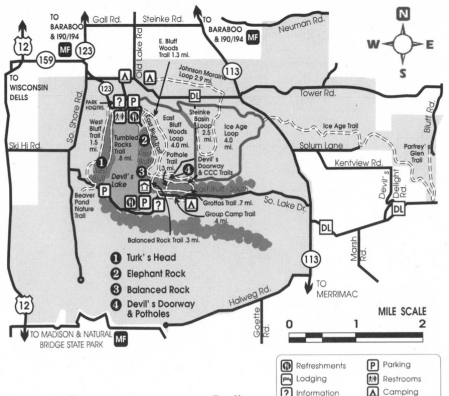

Turk's Head
Elephant Rock
Balanced Rock
Devil's Doorway & Potholes

MILE SCALE

Legend:
- Refreshments
- Lodging
- Information
- Water
- MF Multi-Facilities Available
- Parking
- Restrooms
- Camping
- Shelter
- Mountain Biking Trail
- Hiking Trail
- Roadway

Grottos Trail .7 miles
Easy, wide compacted gravel path along the base of the sound end of the East Bluff.

Ice Age Trail .4 miles
Medium to difficult. Wooded, grassy between Parfrey's Glen and the Ice Age Loop.

Johnson Moraine Loop (White) 2.5 miles
Easy, grassy with variable grades, crosses Hwy. DL twice. There are a number of kettle ponds in the area.

Parfrey's Glen Trail .8 miles
Easy to medium with difficult creek crossings. It follows through a deep gorge and ends at a small waterfall.

Potholes Trail .3 miles
Very difficult, steep climbing trail with stone steps. Provides good views of south areas of park.

Steinke Basin Loop (Green) 2.5 miles
Easy, level grassy, wooded. Runs through an extinct glacial lake bed.

Tumbled Rocks .8 miles
Easy, level asphalt walkway winding through quartzite boulders at the base of West Bluff.

West Bluff Trail (Red) 1.5 miles
Medium effort, asphalt with stone steps and a steep climb on south end and an easier climb up the north end. Crosses the bluff top past drop-offs with scenic views of the lake and park.

Devil's Lake State Park

Harrington Beach State Park

Trail Length	2.0 miles
Effort Level	Easy
Setting	Grass, sand, lake shore
Location	10 miles north of Port Washington on Hwy. 43 and then east on Hwy D for 1 mile.
Information	Harrington Beach State Park 531 Hwy D., Belgium, WI 53004 (414) 285-3015
Comments	The Park consists of 637 acres along the shore of Lake Michigan in Ozaukee County. It is open from 6 am to 11 pm. Biking is allowed along the shuttle bus road. There is a pay phone located beside the lower parking lot.

- Refreshments
- Lodging
- Information
- Water
- MF Multi-Facilities Available

- P Parking
- Restrooms
- Camping
- Shelter

Mountain Biking Trail
Hiking Trail
Roadway

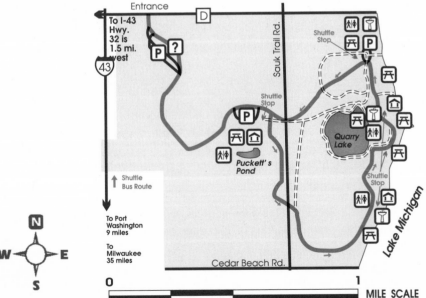

12

Kohler-Andrae State Park

Trail Length   2.5 miles

Effort Level   Easy

Setting   Grassy

Location   4 miles north of Sheboygan on Hwy 43, and then 2 miles east on Park Drive.

Information   Kohler-Andrae State Park
1520 Old Park Rd
Sheboygan, WI 53081
(414) 452-3457

Comments   All park roads are for bicycle use, but they are heavily used. Mountain bikes are not allowed off road or on trails except as designated by signs. In addition to biking, the park offers hiking, nature and horse trails. There are camping, picnic, boating and fishing facilities available.

Black River Trail

To Sheyboygan 5 mi.
To I-43 2.5 mi.

Black River

Kohler Dune Cordwalk

Sanderling Nature Center

Creeping Juniper Nature Trail Loop

State Natural Area

Lake Michigan

Park Office

Entrance
Old Park Rd.

Indian Pipe Nature Trail

?	Information
⌂	Shelter
⊞	Picnic Area
ⵝ	Drinking Fountain
P	Parking
⚹⚹	Restrooms
△	Camping
▬▬	Mountain Biking
= = =	Hiking Trail
▬▬	Roadway

N
W E
S

Kettle Moraine
Northern Unit

IInformation   Kettle Moraine State Forest—North Unit
N1765 Hwy 6
Campbellsport, WI 53010
(414) 626-2116

Northern
Kettle
Moraine

The northern Kettle Moraine offers excellent off-road bicycling. The Greenbush Recreation Area and the New Fane trails are currently open for Mountain Biking, in addition to cross country skiing and hiking. The Zillmer trail is only open to skiing and hiking at this time. These trails have wide mowed grass or forest floor surfaces, and are highlighted on the map.

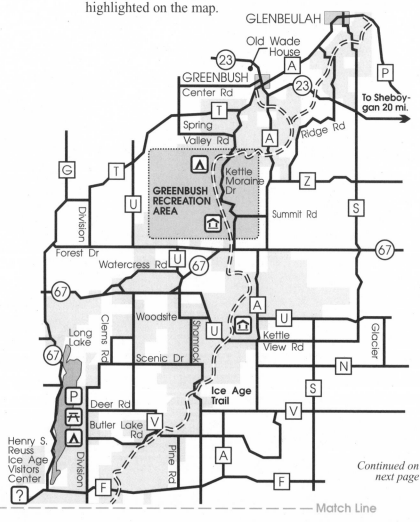

Continued on next page

14

Kettle Moraine State Forest
Bicycling is allowed on designated trails only. The Department of Natural Resources may close a trail if conditions warrant. Mountain Biking is not permitted during the X-C skiing season. Stickers are required for Mountain Biking and skiing, and may be obtained from DNR headquarters offices.

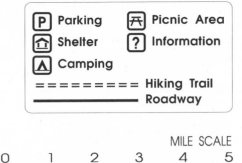

P Parking	**A** Picnic Area
⌂ Shelter	**?** Information
A Camping	

`= = = = = = = =` Hiking Trail
Roadway

MILE SCALE

0   1   2   3   4   5

Continued from previous page

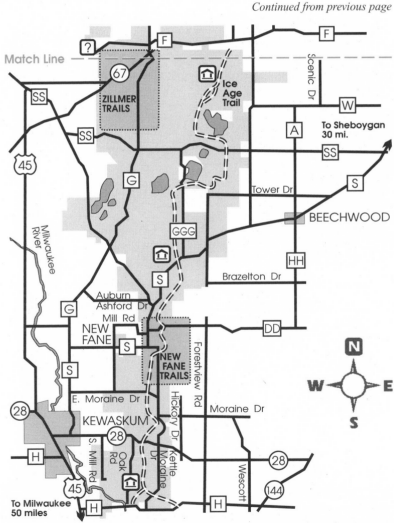

Kettle Moraine - Northern Unit

Greenbush Recreation Area
Kettle Moraine - Northern Unit

Trail Length   10.9 miles (loops)

Effort Level   Easy to Difficult

Setting   Hills, Woods, grassy areas

Location   Hwy. 23 west to Kettle Moraine Drive at the small town of Greenbush. South 2 miles.

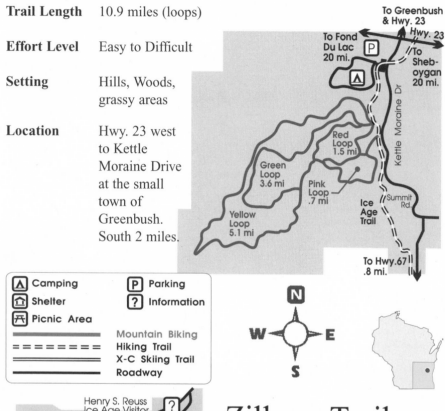

To Greenbush & Hwy. 23

Hwy. 23

To Fond Du Lac 20 mi.

To Sheboygan 20 mi.

Kettle Moraine Dr

Red Loop 1.5 mi

Green Loop 3.6 mi

Pink Loop .7 mi

Summit Rd.

Ice Age Trail

Yellow Loop 5.1 mi

To Hwy.67 .8 mi.

Legend:
- Ⓐ Camping
- ⌂ Shelter
- 🞡 Picnic Area
- Ⓟ Parking
- ⬚? Information
- ─────── Mountain Biking
- = = = = = = = Hiking Trail
- ═══════ X-C Skiing Trail
- ─────── Roadway

N W E S

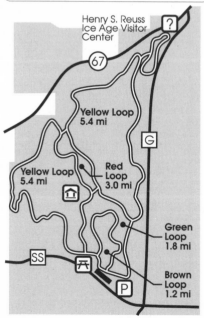

Henry S. Reuss Ice Age Visitor Center ⬚?

67

Yellow Loop 5.4 mi

Ⓖ

Yellow Loop 5.4 mi

Red Loop 3.0 mi

⌂

SS

🞡

Ⓟ

Green Loop 1.8 mi

Brown Loop 1.2 mi

Zillmer Trails
(A hiking or X-C skiing alternate)

Comments   The Zillmer Hiking and X-C Skiing trails lie mainly in deep woods, but offer a mix of wooded and open landscape. Their rolling hills make them an interesting experience. You can climb along the crest of an esker, a narrow sinuous ridge of debris from a river that flowed here during the ice age. The heights provide a great view of the Kettle Moraine and the Dundee Mountain Kame to the northeast.

16

New Fane Trails
Kettle Moraine - Northern Unit

Trail Length 7.7 miles (loops)

Effort Level Easy to Difficult

Setting Hilly, woods, grassy areas

Location From Milwaukee, take Hwy 45 north approx. 35 miles to County Rte. H. East on H for 2 miles to Kettle Moraine Dr., and then north for 3 miles.

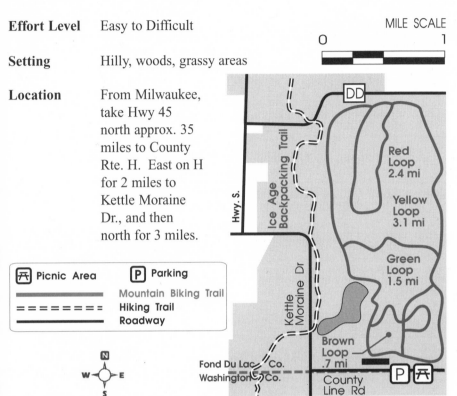

MILE SCALE
0   1

DD

Red Loop 2.4 mi

Yellow Loop 3.1 mi

Green Loop 1.5 mi

Ice Age Backpacking Trail

Hwy. S.

Kettle Moraine Dr

Brown Loop .7 mi

Fond Du Lac Co.
Washington Co.

County Line Rd

🅿 Parking

🏕 Picnic Area

━━━━━ Mountain Biking Trail
= = = = = = = Hiking Trail
━━━━━ Roadway

N
W ─┼─ E
S

RULES OF THE TRAIL

Be courteous to all trail users

Make your presence known well in advance of approach

Wear a helmet

Maintain equipment in excellent working order

Respect "No Trespassing" signs

Always yield the right of way to other trail users

Control your speed at all times

Stay on designated trails

Maintain control of bike at all times

Slow down and pass with care

Don't disturb wildlife or livestock

Pack up litter

Respect public and private property

Know local rules

Plan ahead

Avoid riding in large groups

Minimize impact to surroundings

Report incident of trail impasse to local authorities

Kettle Moraine
Southern Unit

Information   Kettle Moraine State Forest - South Unit
                  S91 W39091 Hwy 59
                  Eagle, WI 53119
                  (414) 594-2135

                  Southern Kettle Moraine Touring Center
                  (414) 495-8600
                  Bicycle rental and service available.

Comments   The John Muir and Emma F. Carlin trails
                  are open to Mountain Biking, Cross
                  Country Skiing, and Hiking. The McMiller
                  Ski Trail is currently limited
                  to Skiing and Hiking. These
                  trail areas are highlighted
                  on the map.

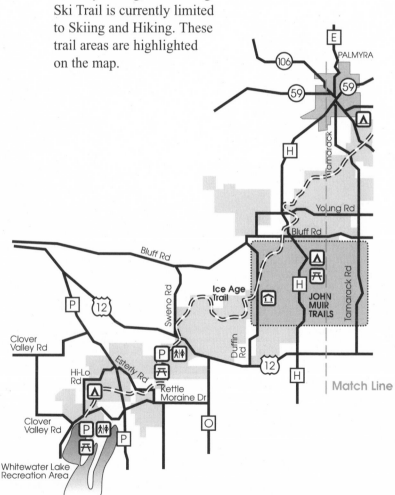

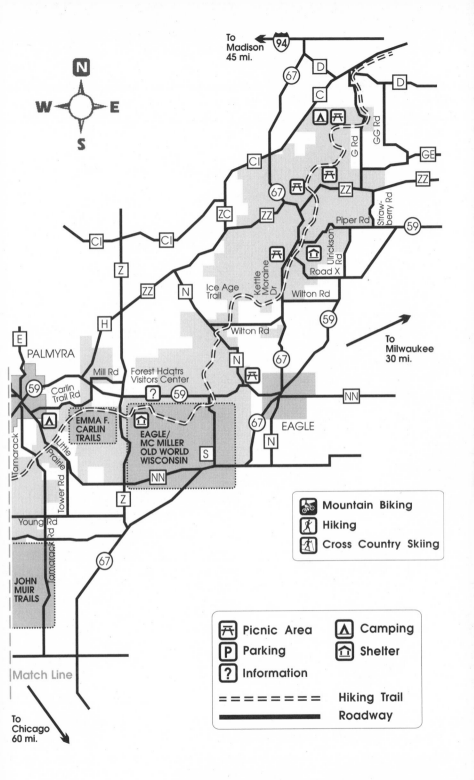

Kettle Moraine - Southern Unit

John Muir Trails
Kettle Moraine - Southern Unit

Trail Length   19.2 miles

Effort Level   Easy to Difficult

Setting   Hilly, rocky, open fields, woods

Location   From Milwaukee, Highway 43 SW to St. Rte 20. West on 20 about 9 miles to where it joins Highway 12. West on Hwy. 12 less than 2 miles to Cnty Rte. H. North on H to entrance. From Chicago, NW on Highway 12.

Comments

Red Loop   This is a good, short, beginner level loop through open fields, scattered pines, and hardwoods. This loop has only one small downhill.

Orange Loop   This loop offers some steep uphill and downhill, but avoids more of the rocky hills and sharp turns that can be encountered when continuing on the Green Loop. There is a downhill that is rather steep near the shelter and should be taken with caution.

Green Loop   Some of the roughest, most diverse sections of the Kettle Moraine will be encountered as you travel this loop. Its steep hills, rocky terrain, and sharp turns make it the most popular with serious mountain bikers.

White Loop   Easy to moderate. The first half of this loop winds through open areas and scattered mature pines. The return half zigzags in and out of hardwood and pine plantations. This loop also provides a view of the forests largest leaf bog.

Blue Loop   Recommended for some great biking. The loop takes you over 3 miles deep into mature hardwood forest. They say don't miss the spring display of Jack-in-the-pulpits.

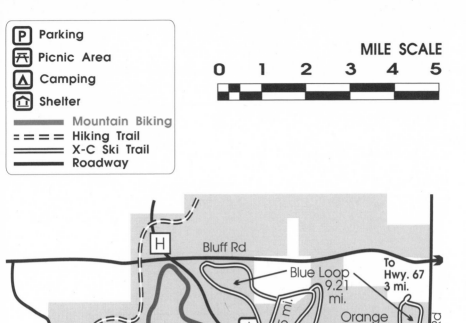

Map Legend

- **P** Parking
- **⊼** Picnic Area
- **△** Camping
- **⌂** Shelter

━━━ Mountain Biking
= = = = Hiking Trail
═══ X-C Ski Trail
━━━ Roadway

MILE SCALE

0 1 2 3 4 5

Bluff Rd

Blue Loop 9.21 mi.

To Hwy. 67 3 mi.

Orange Loop 3.1 mi.

Red Loop 2.5 mi.

Green Loop 4.3 mi.

Green Loop 7.4 mi

Red Loop 2.0 mi

Orange Loop 4.8 mi

Ice Age Trail

Duffin Rd

Tamarack Rd

Blue Loop 10 mi.

White Loop 3.2 mi.

To Hwy. 12 1 mi.

White Loop 4 mi.

N
W — E
S

Shelters are available to backpackers using the Ice Age Trail. Three reservable, overnight backpacking shelters are available year-round. Each shelter is an open front, Adirondack-style lean-to with an earth floor. The shelter areas include a latrine, fire pit, and additional tenting space.

John Muir Trails

Emma F. Carlin Trails
Kettle Moraine - Southern Unit

Trail Length 9.4 miles (loops) **Setting** Hilly, woods

Effort Level Easy to Difficult **Location** From Milwaukee, Hwy 43 SW approx. 20 miles to town of Mukwonago. Pick up Cnty Rte. NN north of town and proceed west 5 miles to Eagle. Continue west on St Rte 59 for 4 miles to Carlin Trail Rd. South to entrance.

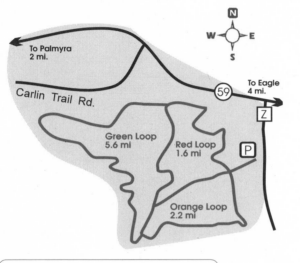

To Palmyra 2 mi.

Carlin Trail Rd.

To Eagle 4 mi.

59

Z

P

Green Loop 5.6 mi

Red Loop 1.6 mi

Orange Loop 2.2 mi

🏠 Shelter   P Parking
❓ Information
====== Hiking Trail
X-C Skiing Trail
Roadway

Eagle/ McMiller Old World Wisconsin Areas

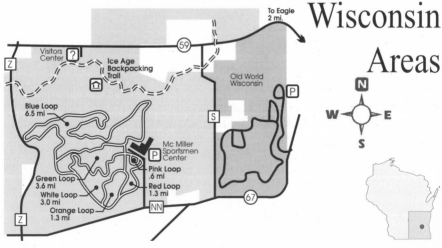

To Eagle 2 mi.

Visitors Center ❓

Z

Ice Age Backpacking Trail

59

Old World Wisconsin

P

Blue Loop 6.5 mi

S

Mc Miller Sportsmen Center

P

Green Loop 3.6 mi

Pink Loop .6 mi

White Loop 3.0 mi

Red Loop 1.3 mi

Orange Loop 1.3 mi

NN

67

Z

Lapham Peak Unit
Kettle Moraine State Forest

Trail Length	4.4 miles
Effort Level	Easy to Difficult
Setting	Hills, woods, fields
Location	7 miles west of Waukesha on Hwy 94, and then south 1 mile on County Hwy C.
Information	Lapham Peak N846 W329 Cth C Delefield, WI 53018 (414) 896-8007

Ⓜ Refreshments　Ⓟ Parking
❓ Information　⟨ⵜ⟩ Restrooms
🎋 Picnic Area　Ⓐ Camping
🍷 Drinking Fountain　⌂ Shelter
▬▬▬ Mountain Bike Trail
= = = = = = Hiking Trail
━━━━━ Roadway

Comments　Lapham Peak is a unit of the Kettle Moraine State Forest. In addition to biking, there are miles of hiking and ski trails winding through wooded hills and fields. The 45 foot observation tower provides a beautiful view, and there are picnic facilities near its base.

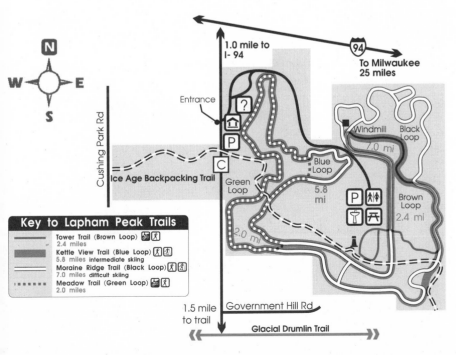

SOUTH WEST
Mountain Biking Trails

Blue Mound State Park 26

Wildcat Mountain State Park 27

Governor Dodge State Park 28

Mirror Lake State Park 30

Perrot State Park 31

Wyalusing State Park 32

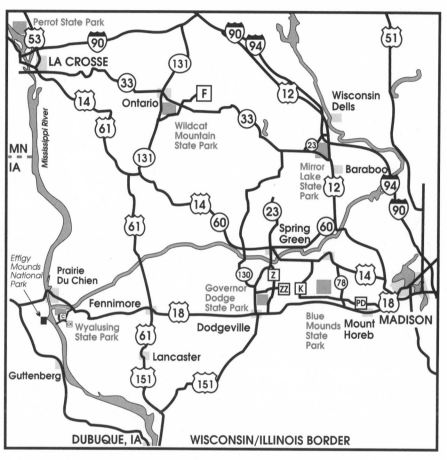

Perrot State Park
53 90
90
94
51
LA CROSSE
131
33
131
14
Ontario
F
12
Wisconsin
Dells
61
33
33
MN
IA
Wildcat
Mountain
State Park
23
131
Mirror
Lake
State
Park
Baraboo
94
14
60
12
90
61
23
60
Spring
Green
Effigy
Mounds
National
Park
Prairie
Du Chien
130
Z
14
Fennimore
ZZ
K
78
MADISON
18
PD
18
Wyalusing
State Park
Governor
Dodge
State Park
Dodgeville
Blue
Mounds
State
Park
Mount
Horeb
61
Guttenberg
Lancaster
151
151
DUBUQUE, IA
WISCONSIN/ILLINOIS BORDER

——— Mountain Biking trail

- - - Leisure Biking trail

=== Cross-Country Skiing

⋯⋯ Snowmobile trail

=== Hiking Trail

➖➖ Horseback Riding Trail

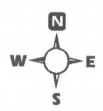

Area Overview

25

Blue Mound State Park

Effort Level   Easy to Difficult

Setting   Grass, woods, steep hills

Location   1 mile northwest of the town of Blue Mounds off Hwy 18/51

Information   Blue Mounds State Park
PO Box 98
Blue Mounds, WI 53517
(608) 437-5711

Comments   The Park is the highest point in Southern Wisconsin at 1,716
feet, and is located about 25 miles west of Madison. In
addition to some great biking, take advantage of the Park's
nature program, heated outdoor swimming pool, picnic
facilities, observation towers and hiking trails.

Area Attractions:

Mt. Horeb - Locally crafted products and art pieces, antique shops.

Cave of the Mounds - Guided underground cave tour. Admission charge.

Little Norway - Guided tour of a pioneer Norwegian homestead built in the 1850's.
Admission charge.

Song of Norway - Outdoor performance at the Cave of the Mounds
life of the Norwegian composer,
Grieg. Admission charge.

Wisconsin Folk Museum-
Exhibits of regional folk art.
Donation.

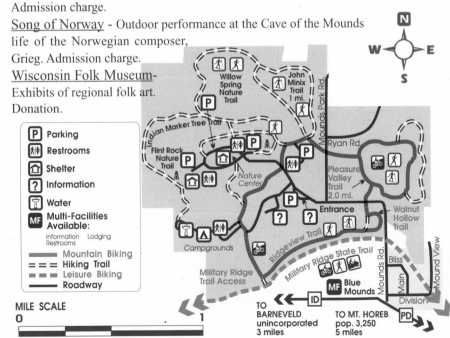

Wildcat Mountain State Park

Trail Length   Park roads

Effort Level   Easy

Setting   Woods, hills, bluffs, river valley

Location: From the town of Ontario, 2 miles south on Hwy 131. Ontario is approximately 45 miles east of LaCrosse.

Information: (608) 337-4775

Comments: Wildcat Mountain State Park is located in the unglaciated Kickapoo Valley. The 3,500 acre park provides picnic areas, a seven mile cross country ski trail, hiking and horse trails. Highlights include canoeing on the Kickapoo River and the Scenery at Observation Point. Its hills, made up of Precambrian sandstone, have many exposed bluffs. Much of this area is a refuge to white tailed deer, grouse, raccoon, rabbit, mink, turtles, otters, red and gray squirrels, butterflies, salamanders and various songbirds. *Biking is limited to park roads, and is not allowed on hiking or horse trails.*

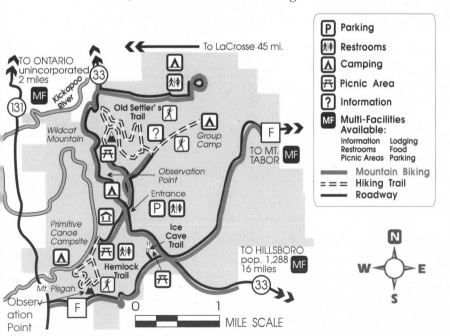

Governor Dodge State Park

Trail Length   10 miles

Effort Level   Difficult

Setting   Meadows, wooded ridges and valleys

Location   3 miles north of Dodgeville on Hwy 23

Information   Governor Dodge State Park
R.R. 1, Box 42
Dodgeville, WI 53533
(608) 935-2315

Comments   Governor Dodge is the second largest state park in Wisconsin.
The terrain in the park is rugged and varies from steep hills
and sandstone bluffs to deep lush valleys. Activities include
hiking, horseback riding, swimming, picnicking and camping.
Meadow Valley Trail and Mill Creek Trail are the two
designated off road biking trails. These trails are shared
with hikers. The Mill Creek Trail provides access to the
Military Ridge State Trail.

Meadow Valley Trail

A 6.8 mile loop trail beginning at the Cox Hollow Beach
picnic area. The trail follows along the ridge of the Lost
Canyon and passes through open
meadows and wooded ridges.

Mill Creek Trail

A 3.3 mile loop trail beginning at the Cox
Hollow Beach picnic area. The trail
winds through meadows and wooded
valleys.

Hiking Trails:
Gold Mine Trail .... 2.50 miles
Lost Canyon Trail .... 8.10 miles
Stephens Falls Trail .... .25 miles

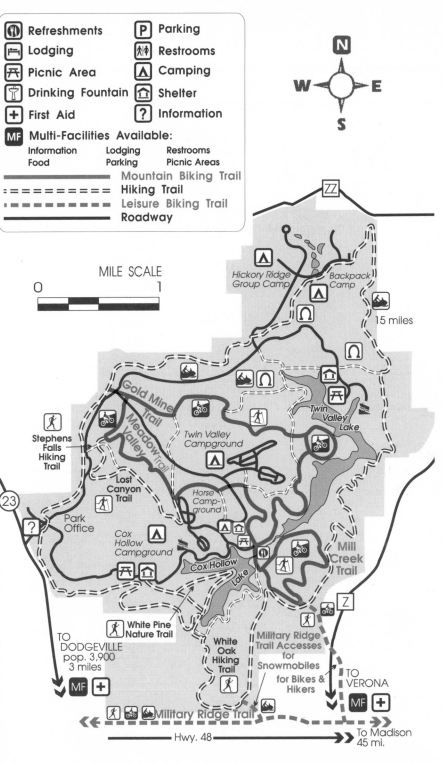

Governor Dodge State Park

Mirror Lake State Park

Trail Length   9.2 miles

Effort Level   Easy to Moderate

Setting   Woods, gravel, sand

Location   1.5 miles southwest of Lake Delton on Ishnala Road. Exit Hwy. 94 at Hwy. 12 and proceed south for 1 mile to Fern Dell Road. There is an entrance at the Hastings Road intersection on the northwest side with parking and information facilities.

Information   Mirror Lake State Park
E10320 Fern Dell Road
Baraboo, WI 53913
(608) 254-2333

Comments   The Park's off-road bike trails are limited to the south portion of the park, and are not developed. Be cautious of loose gravel, sand and wet leaves. All campsites have toilets, picnic areas and water. Showers and electrified campsites are available.

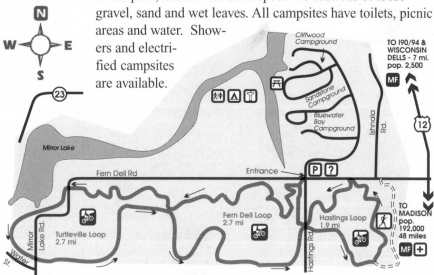

Perrot State Park

Trail Length   6 miles

Effort Level   Moderate to Difficult

Setting   Hardpacked ski trials. Marshland, prairie, wooded slopes.

Location   From LaCrosse, take Hwy 35 north and then west to Hwy 93 at Centerville. South on 93 for 4.5 miles to Trempealeau. Follow park signs. From Winona, cross Hwy 43 bridge and take Hwy 35 east 10 miles to Centerville.

Information   Perrot State Park
Route 1, Box 407
Trempealeau, WI 54661
(608) 534-6409

Comments

Perrot State Park offers a diverse mix of terrain, from marshland, valleys, dry prairies to upland fields and densely wooded bluffs. Brady's Bluff, at 500-feet, provides great views of the Mississippi. Mountain biking is allowed based on conditions. Nicholas Perrot wintered in the area in 1685-86 prior to claiming all the land west of the Great Lakes for France. The Park has many campsites, picnic areas, overlooks, and miles of trails for alternate uses. There is water and restrooms at the trailhead as well as at most camp-sites and picnic areas.

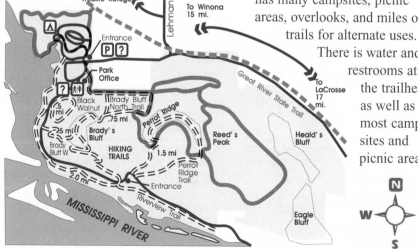

Wyalusing State Park

Trail Length   11.6 miles

Effort Level   Easy to Difficult

Setting   Woods, grassy areas, gently rolling to steep slopes.

Location   7 miles south of Prairie Du Chien on Hwy 18, then west on Hwy C

Information   Wyalusing State Park
13342 County Hwy C
Bradley, WI   53801
(608) 996-2261

Comments   Bicycling is allowed on park roads and designated trails.

Mississippi Ridge Trail

3.6 miles - Moderate. Few slopes, gently rolling. The trail winds along heavily wooded ridge tops above the Mississippi River to the Mississippi River View Picnic Area, then returns up Cathedral Tree Drive.

Sand Cave Trail

1.7 miles - Moderate. Steep slopes, drop-offs, some steps. Heavily wooded. The trail winds past a small creek with a waterfall and colorful Sand Cave.

Turkey Hollow Trail

3.2 miles - Easy. Wide, grassy, gentle slopes. Partly wooded, rolling trail through planted pines, open fields, oak hardwoods and brushlands.

Whitetail Meadows Trail

3.2 miles - Easy. Grassy. The trail is gently rolling and follows along the edge between open meadows and woodlands. Turkeys and deer are often viewed.

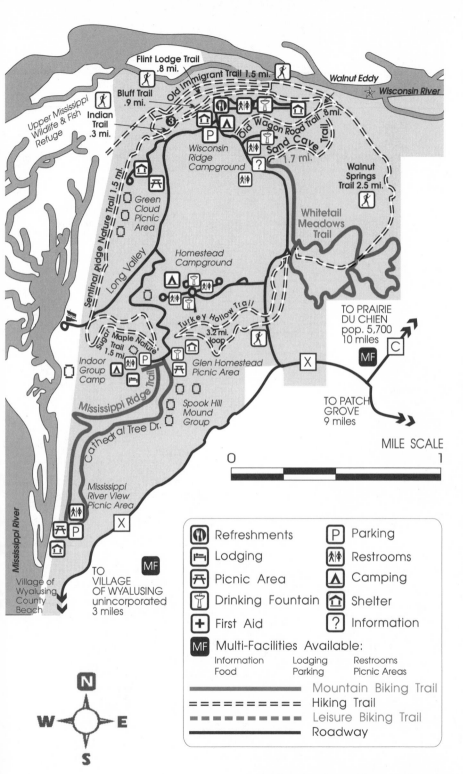

Wyalusing State Park

NORTH EAST
Mountain Biking Trails

High Cliff State Park.. 36

Oconto County Trail 38

Newport State Park 40

Door County Overview... 41

Peninsula State Park 42

Potawantomi State Park 44

Point Beach State Park... 46

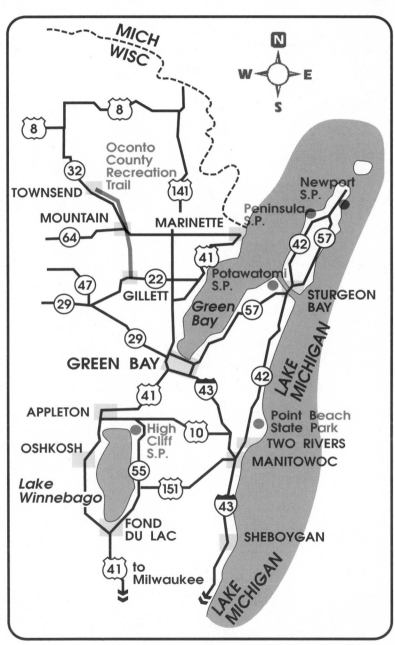

American Bike Trails

MICH
WISC

N
W ← → E
S

8
8
Oconto County Recreation Trail
32
TOWNSEND
141
MOUNTAIN
MARINETTE
64
41
Newport S.P.
Peninsula S.P.
42 57
22
Potawatomi S.P.
47
GILLETT
29
Green Bay
57
STURGEON BAY
29
GREEN BAY
42
41
43
LAKE MICHIGAN
APPLETON
High Cliff S.P.
10
Point Beach State Park
OSHKOSH
TWO RIVERS
55
MANITOWOC
Lake Winnebago
151
43
FOND DU LAC
SHEBOYGAN
41
to Milwaukee
LAKE MICHIGAN

Area Overview

35

High Cliff State Park

Trail Length   8.2 miles

Effort Level   Easy

Setting   Woods, cliffs, lakefront

Location   3 miles south on Hwy. 55 from the town of Sherwood. At High Cliff Rd. turn left to enter park. Sherwood is approximately 12 miles southeast of Appleton.

Information   High Cliff State Park
N7475 High Cliff Rd.
Menasha, WI 54952
(414) 989-1349

Comments   The High Cliff escarpment rises 223 feet above Lake Winnebago, providing a sweeping view of this 215 square mile lake and the surrounding country. The park is the site of prehistoric Indians known as the Effigy Mound Indians. They built mounds measuring 25 to 285 feet in length, and which are still seen between the quarry and the camp-grounds. The park has a good variety of plants for the nature lover and small animal life is common.

Bicycling is allowed only on paved roads and marked bicycle trails.

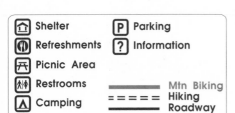

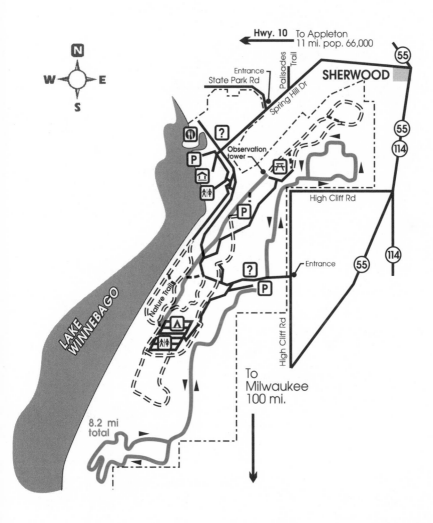

To Appleton
11 mi. pop. 66,000

Hwy. 10

SHERWOOD

Entrance
State Park Rd

Observation
tower

High Cliff Rd

Entrance

To
Milwaukee
100 mi.

LAKE WINNEBAGO

Nature Trail

8.2 mi
total

Palisades Trail

Spring Hill Dr

High Cliff Rd

High Cliff State Park

Oconto County Trail

Trail Length 30 miles

Effort Level Easy

Setting Abandoned railbed. Forests, farmland, small communities.

Location Gillett north to Townsend. Gillett is located 14 miles west of Hwy. 141 on Hwy. 22, and is approximately 42 miles northwest of Green Bay.

Information Oconto Forests & Parks
Oconto County Courthouse
300 Washington St.
Oconto, WI 54153
(414) 834-6820

Comments The Oconto County Recreation Trail runs from Gillett to Townsend on an abandoned railroad grade through out the Nicolet National Forest. In addition to the trail there are many roads suitable for mountain biking. Oconto County borders the western side of Green Bay.

P	Parking	**⛱**	Picnic Area
?	Information	**👫**	Restrooms

━━━━━━━━━ Mtn. Biking
========= Hiking
━━━━━━━━━ Roadway

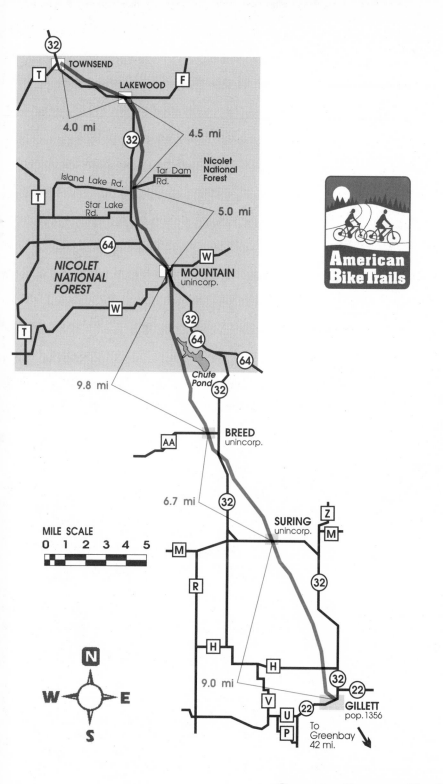

Oconto County Trail

Newport State Park

Trail Length   12 miles

Effort Level   Easy

Setting   Forests, wetlands, meadows.

Location   Door County. 2 miles east of Ellison Bay on Hwy 22, and then 2 miles SE on Hwy Z

Information   (414) 854-2500

Comments   Newport State Park has 2,400 acres. It's 11 miles of undeveloped shoreline are noted for clean sandy beaches, hidden coves, and rocky headlands.

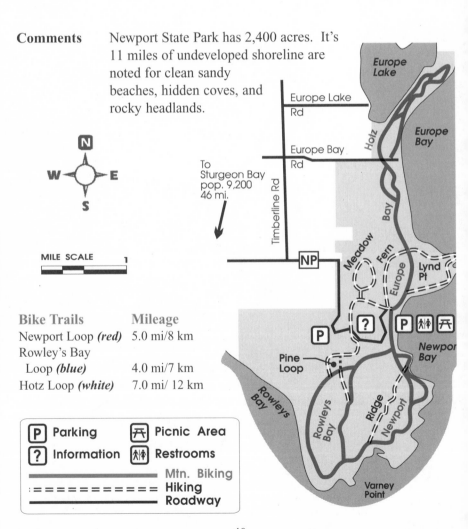

Bike Trails	Mileage
Newport Loop *(red)*	5.0 mi/8 km
Rowley's Bay Loop *(blue)*	4.0 mi/7 km
Hotz Loop *(white)*	7.0 mi/ 12 km

P Parking   ⌐Ħ Picnic Area
? Information   ⋔⋔ Restrooms
───── Mtn. Biking
========= Hiking
───── Roadway

Door County

EMERGENCY ASSISTANCE   - DIAL 911
Medical Services:
D.C. Medical Center   - 414/746-1020
Nor-Door Clinic   - 414/854-2347
Door County Memorial Hosp.   - 800/522-8919
HELP of Door County   - 414/743-8818

Door County's varied landscape and roadways make it ideal for bicycle touring. The Backroad Bicycle Route is a 100 MILE ride through fields and forests on country roads and byways. It links the small towns along both coasts. Biking is at its best in the late spring and early fall.

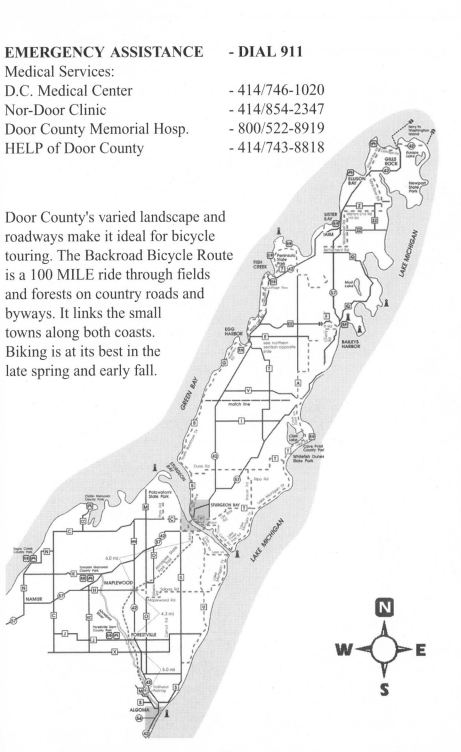

Peninsula State Park

Trail Length 12.8 miles

Effort Level Easy to moderate

Setting Forest, meadows, marsh, cliffs.

Location Door County. 3 miles north of Fish Creek off Hwy. 42.

Information Peninsula State Park
P.O. Box 218
Fish Creek, WI 54212
(414) 868-3258

Comments Peninsula State Park has 3,763 acres of forest, dolomite cliffs, marshland and meadows. Park roads are narrow and heavily traveled. Use of the Sunset Bike Trail and back roads is encouraged. Many of the roads have steep downgrades with corners and intersections. Ride single file, under full control, be prepared to stop and wear safety attire.

Eagle Bluff Lighthouse

On the National Register of Historic Places. It was built in 1868 and has been restored. Located in Peninsula State Park between Fish Creek and Ephraim.

American Bike Trails

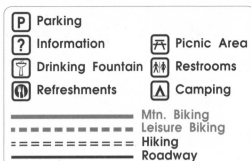

P Parking
? Information
🍴 Drinking Fountain
🥤 Refreshments

🎪 Picnic Area
🚻 Restrooms
⛺ Camping

———— Mtn. Biking
– – – – – Leisure Biking
= = = = = Hiking
———— Roadway

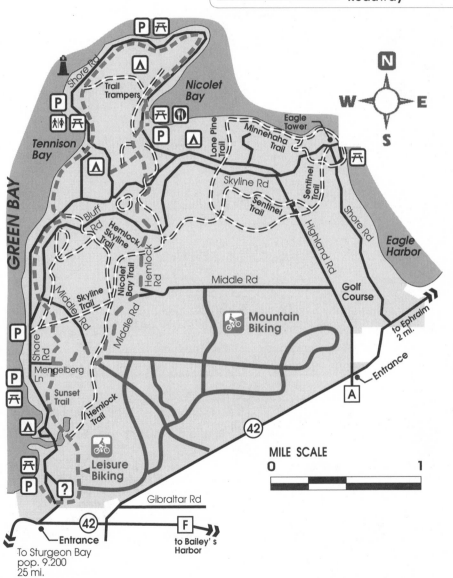

Shore Rd

Trail Trampers

Nicolet Bay

Eagle Tower

Minnehaha Trail

Lone Pine Trail

Tennison Bay

GREEN BAY

Skyline Rd

Sentinel Trail

Sentinel Trail

Bluff Rd

Hemlock Skyline Trail

Shore Rd

Eagle Harbor

Skyline Trail

Nicolet Bay Trail

Hemlock Rd

Middle Rd

Highland Rd

Middle Rd

Middle Rd

Golf Course

🚴 Mountain Biking

Mengelberg Ln

Sunset Trail

Hemlock Trail

🚴 Leisure Biking

to Ephraim 2 mi.

Entrance

A

42

MILE SCALE

0   1

Gibraltar Rd

42

F

Entrance

to Bailey's Harbor

To Sturgeon Bay
pop. 9.200
25 mi.

Peninsula State Park

Potawatomi State Park

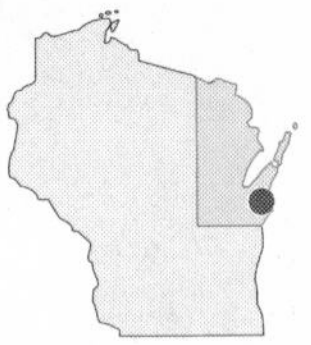

Trail Length 4 miles

Effort Level Moderate

Setting Flat to gently rolling upland terrain, borderd by steep slopes and cliffs.

Location Door County. 5 miles northwest of Sturgeon Bay. Take Hwy. 42/57 west to Park Rd., and then north to park entrance.

Information Potawatomi State Park
3740 Park Dr.
Sturgeon Bay, WI 54235
(414) 746-2890

Comments Potawatomi State Park has nearly 1,200 acres of flat to gently rolling upland terrain bordered by steep slopes and rugged limestone cliffs along the Sturgeon Bay shoreline. The observation tower atop a limestone bluff offers a majestic view of Sawyer harbor.

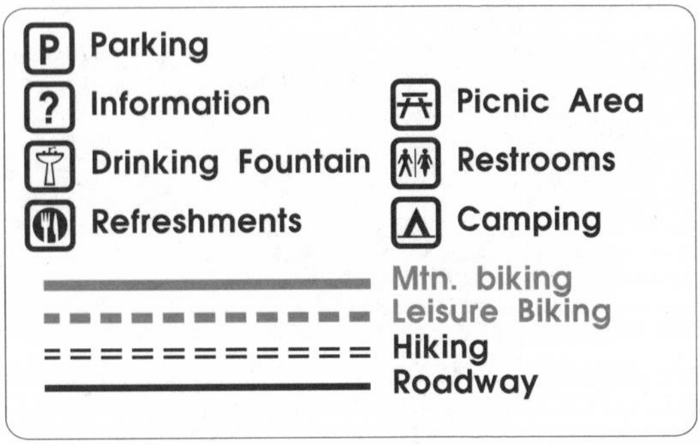
Parking
Information
Picnic Area
Drinking Fountain
Restrooms
Refreshments
Camping
Mtn. biking
Leisure Biking
Hiking
Roadway

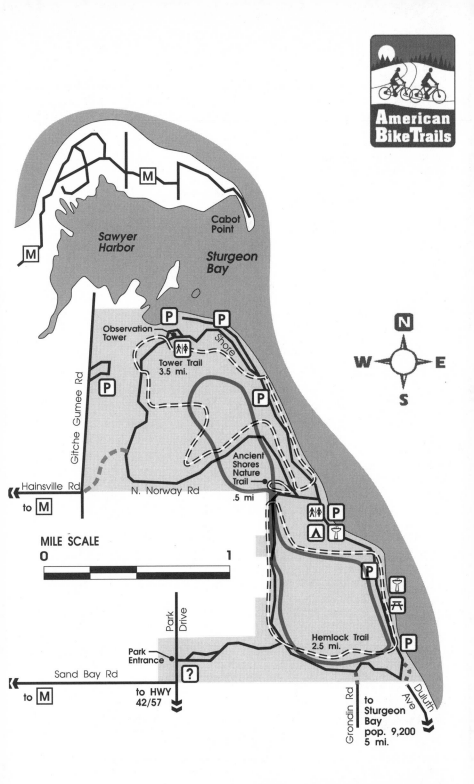

Potawatomi State Park

Point Beach State Forest

Trail Length   4 miles

Effort Level   Moderate

Setting   Forest bordered by sand beaches.

Location   4 miles north of Two Rivers, off County Hwy O.

Information   Point Beach State Park
9400 County Hwy. O
Two Rivers, WI   54241
(414) 794-7480

Comments   Point Beach State Forest has more than 2,800 acres of forest lands bordered on the east by six miles of sand beach on Lake Michigan. Mountain biking is limited to the Red Pine Trail. The trail begins at the parking lot which is located west of Hwy. 0, directly across from the entrance road. In addition to biking, there are some 11 miles of hiking/ski trails through woods and dunes. A 113 foot high lighthouse at Rawley Point is operated by the Coast Guard. No tours are available, but bring your camera and photograph it from the beach.

P Parking	**⚓** Lighthouse
? Information	**⊞** Picnic Area
🚰 Drinking Fountain	**🚻** Restrooms
🍴 Refreshments	**△** Camping

Mtn. biking
▬▬▬▬▬ Snowmobiling
========= Hiking
▬▬▬▬▬ Roadway

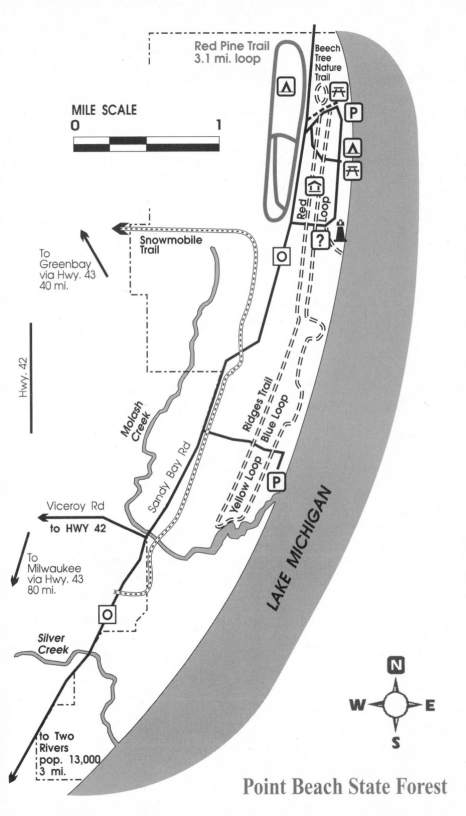

MILE SCALE

Red Pine Trail
3.1 mi. loop

Beech
Tree
Nature
Trail

To
Greenbay
via Hwy. 43
40 mi.

Snowmobile
Trail

Red Loop

Hwy. 42

Molash Creek

Sandy Bay Rd

Ridges Trail

Blue Loop

Yellow Loop

Viceroy Rd
to HWY 42

To
Milwaukee
via Hwy. 43
80 mi.

LAKE MICHIGAN

Silver
Creek

to Two
Rivers
pop. 13,000
3 mi.

N
W   E
S

Point Beach State Forest

WEST CENTRAL
Mountain Biking Trails

Black River State Forest 50

      Castle Mound Park 52

      Pigeon Creek 53

      Smrekar 54

      Wildcat 54

Lake Wissota State Park 56

Lowes Creek County Park 58

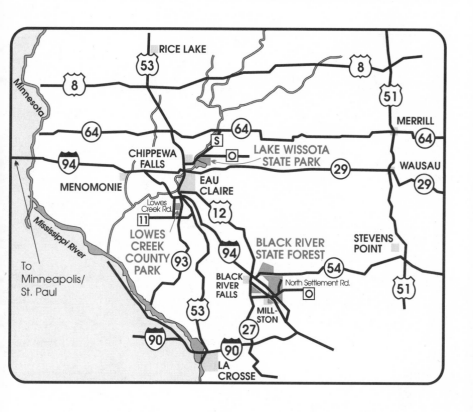

Area Overview

Black River State Forest

Information:
Black River State Forest
    910 Hwy 54 East
    Black River Falls,
    WI 54615
    (715) 284-1400

Comments:
Black River State Forest consists of approximately 66,000 acres located on the edge of the glaciated central plain east of the driftless area of Wisconsin. Its rising sandstone ridges, isolated bluffs and scenic beauty is also ideal for hiking and backpacking. The Black River and its east fork can provide good canoeing in the spring and summer. There are campgrounds and picnic sites at Castle Mound, Pigeon Creek and East Fork. Mountain biking is allowed on the 24 miles of cross-country ski trails, and there are numerous blacktop roads available as bikeways throughout the forest.

EMERGENCY ASSISTANCE
Your first contact in an emergency should be the park office. If no one is available, dial 911, giving details and your location within the park.

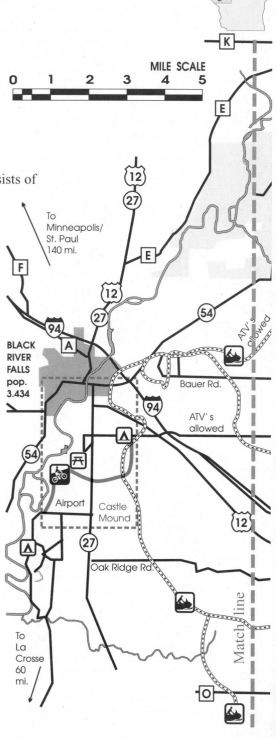

MILE SCALE

0 1 2 3 4 5

To Minneapolis/ St. Paul 140 mi.

BLACK RIVER FALLS pop. 3.434

Bauer Rd.

ATV's allowed

Airport

Castle Mound

Oak Ridge Rd.

To La Crosse 60 mi.

Matchline

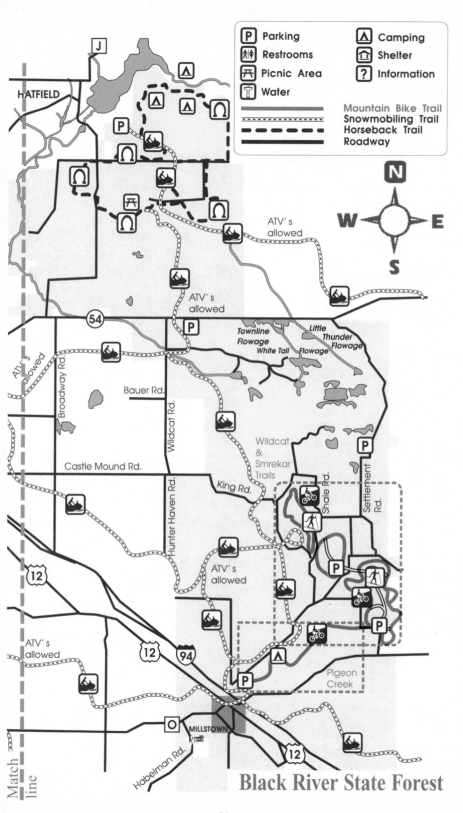

Black River State Forest

Castle Mound Park

Trail Length: 4.5 miles

Effort Level: Easy

Setting: Generally level with grassy surface, but some hills.

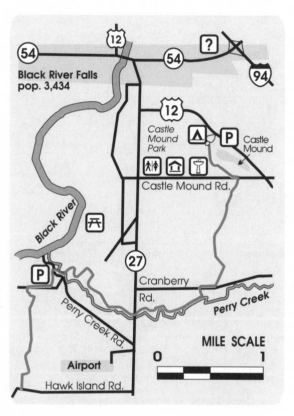

Location:
1.5 miles southeast of Black River Falls on Hwy. 12.

Comments:
The trail is mainly grass and runs from Castle Mound southwest to Hawk Island Road. The terrain is fairly level, but some hills will be encountered near Perry Creek. There is parking at Castle Mound and Perry Creek Road.

? Information		P Parking
Picnic Area		Restrooms
Drinking Fountain		Camping
MF Multi-Facilities Available:		Shelter
Information Lodging Restrooms		
Food Parking Picnic		

Mountain Biking
Roadway

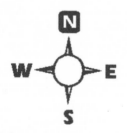

Pigeon Creek

Trail Length: 4 miles

Effort Level: Easy

Setting: Fairly level terrain with mostly grassy surface.

Location: 12 miles southeast of Black River Falls on Hwy 12 to Hwy. 0; then 4 miles northeast to North Settlement Road. Parking available.

Comments: The trail is grass surfaced, except for the last mile which is packed dirt. It runs along fairly level terrain. One section connects you to the Smrekar ski trail parking lot, while the section going westward connects you to North Settlement Road, which will take you back to Pigeon Creek campground or to the town of Millston.

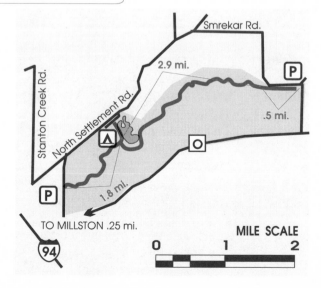

P Parking   A Camping

Mountain Bike Trail
Roadway

American Bike Trails

53

Smrekar Trail

Trail Length: 7.5 miles

Effort Level: Moderate to difficult

Setting: Wooded, ridges.

Location: 12 miles southeast of Black River Falls on Hwy. 12 to Hwy 0; then 4 miles northeast to North Settlement Road. Continue northeast.

Comments: Your biking starts from the Wildcat parking lot. Proceed east, crossing North Settlement Road. Turn right at the trail intersection. The area is wooded, with views of nearby bluffs. The Ridge Trail is difficult and strenuous, but it takes you to the top of the ridge from which to enjoy beautiful, panoramic views.

Wildcat Trail

Trail Length: 7.5 miles

Effort Level: Moderate to difficult

Setting: Heavy woods, buttes and sandstone hills

Location: 12 miles southeast of Black River Falls on Hwy. 12 to Hwy. 0; then 4 miles northeast to North Settlement Road. Continue northeast.

Comments: Enter the trail from the northwest side of the Wildcat parking lot, which is accessed from Old Settlement Road and is about .8 miles north of Smrekar Road. The area is heavily wooded. Take the opportunity to seek out some of the very spectacular views of buttes and sandstone hills.

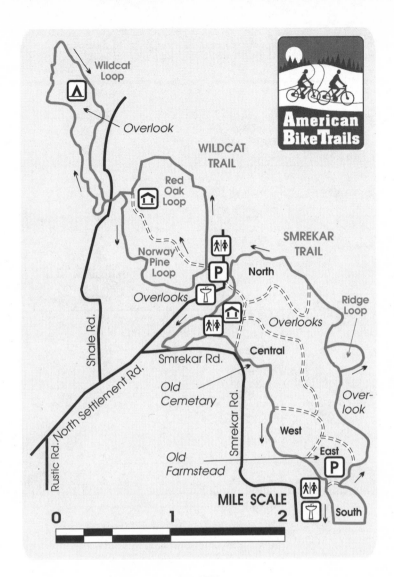

Smrekar Trail & Wildcat Trail

Lake Wissota State Park

Trail Length: 11 miles

Effort Level: Easy

Setting: Mostly prairie grass and plantation pines.

Location: 8 miles northeast of Chippewa Falls. Go north on Hwy. 53, then east on County Road 3. Turn right (east) on County Road S and continue 1.7 miles to park entrance.

Information: Lake Wissota State Park R.R. 8, Box 360 Chippewa Falls, WI 54729 (715) 382-4574

Comments: Lake Wissota was created when settlers damned the river at Chippewa Falls. It's situated on a plain formed from deposits of the ancient Chippewa River.

The park has two trail systems available for mountain biking. The Horse Trail is five miles long and the effort easy. The Pine, Plantation, Eagle Prairie and Jack Pine Trails total 6 miles and the effort is also easy. The Staghorn and Lake Trail as well as the Nature Trail are closed to biking.

TO CHIPPEWA FALLS **MF** pop. 12,727 4.5 miles

P PARK OFFICE **?**

Plantation Trail .8 mi

P Overlook Lake Trail 1.4 mi.

Lake Wissota

Match line

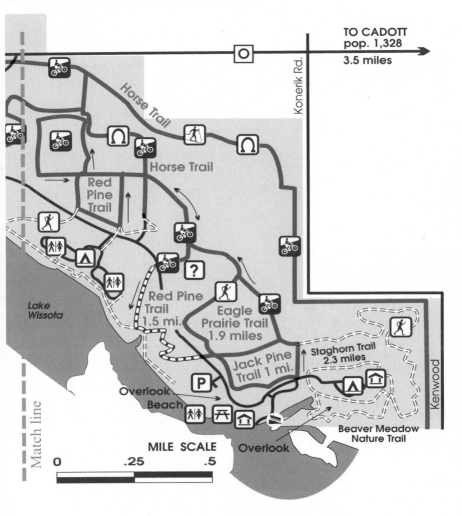

Lake Wissota State Park

Lowes Creek County Park

Trail Length: 4.9 miles

Effort Level: Easy to difficult

Setting: The West Loop is rolling and prairie.
The East Loop is wooded.
The trail loop between the East and West Loop is flat and mostly open.

Location: 1.3 miles west of Hwy. 93 on Hwy. 94 to Lowes Creek Road; then south 1.5 miles to park entrance.

Information: Parks and Forest Dept.
Eau Claire County
227 1st Street West
Altoona, WI 54720
(715) 839-4738

? Information		**P** Parking	
☖ Picnic Area		**⚥** Restrooms	
⚱ Drinking Fountain		**⛺** Camping	
MF Multi-Facilities Available:		**⌂** Shelter	

Information   Lodging   Restrooms
Food   Parking   Picnic

▬▬▬▬ Mountain Biking
▬▬▬▬ Roadway

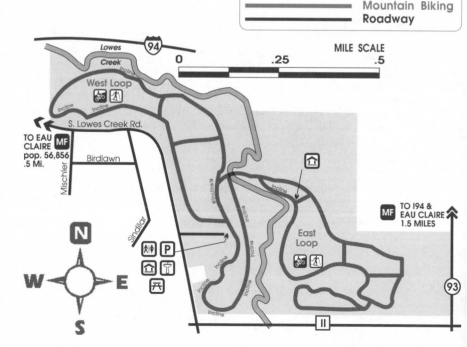

FACILITIES

🔧	Bicycle Service
🔺	Camping
🛶	Canoe Launch
➕	First Aid
❓	Information/Park Office
🛏	Lodging
🅿	Parking
🪑	Picnic Area
🍸	Refreshments
🚻	Restrooms
🏠	Shelter
🚰	Water
MF	**Multi-Facilities Available**

First Aid   Lodging
Picnic   Refreshments
Restrooms   Telephone

TRAIL TYPES

▬▬	Mountain Biking trail
▪ ▪ ▪	Leisure Biking trail
＝＝	Cross-Country Skiing
⋯⋯	Snowmobile trail
= = =	Hiking Trail
▬ ▬	Horseback Riding Trail

TRAIL USES

🚵	Mountain biking
🚴	Leisure biking
⛷	Cross-Country Skiing
🛷	Snowmobiling
🚶	Hiking
🧲	Horseback riding

AREA DESCRIPTION

⬜	Park
⬛	Waterway
▢	Marsh
▬	Mile scale
✛	Directional

ROADS

▬▬	Street
🛡45	Interstate Highway
45	U.S. Highway
45	State Highway
JJ	County Highway

NORTH CENTRAL
Mountain Biking Trails

Council Grounds State Park 62

Hiawatha Trail 64

Lumberjack Trail 66

Madeline Lake Trail 68

McNaughton Lake Trail 69

Nine-Mile County Forest 70

Shannon Lake Trail 72

Chequamegon National Forest 73

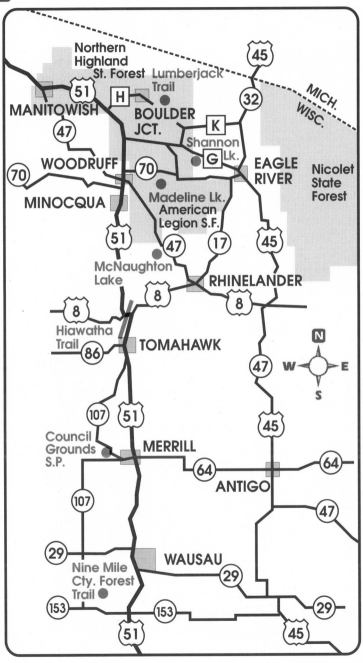

Area Overview

Council Grounds State Park

Trail Length   2.5 miles

Effort Level   Easy

Setting   Heavily wooded

Location   1 mile west of Merrill on Hwy. 107.

Information   Council Grounds State Park
1110 E. 10th St.
Merrill, WI 54452
(715) 536-8773

Comments   Council Grounds State Park receives over 200,000 recreational visitors a year. In addition to the off-road trail, the park roads are open to biking, but most are one-way. They are narrow, well traveled and follow the terrain which has some steep downgrades with corners and intersections. Wildlife is frequently seen along the trails, including squirrel, deer, raccoon, songbirds, and even red fox.

The name Council Grounds was based on stories that the Chippewa Indians once used the site for their annual councils and festivals. They would travel down the Wisconsin River each year for several days of celebration.

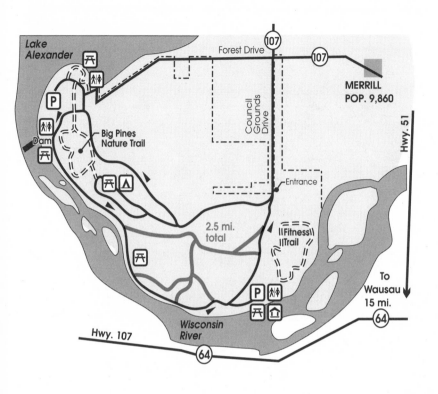

Lake
Alexander

Forest Drive

107

107

MERRILL
POP. 9,860

P

Council
Grounds
Drive

Hwy. 51

Big Pines
Nature Trail

Dam

Entrance

2.5 mi.
total

Fitness
Trail

P

P

To
Wausau
15 mi.

64

Wisconsin
River

Hwy. 107

64

MILE SCALE
0   1

N
W   E
S

P Parking   ‖‖ Restrooms
⌂ Shelter   ? Information
━━━━━━━━━━ Mtn. Biking
= = = = = = = = = Hiking
━━━━━━━━━━ Roadway

Council Grounds State Park

Hiawatha Trail

Trail Length   6.6 miles

Effort Level   Easy

Setting   Abandoned railroad bed. Open areas, woods, farmland.

Location   From the junction of Hwy. 51 and 86 in Tomahawk, west on
Somo Ave. to Sara Park Activity Center and the south
trailhead.

Information   Tomahawk Chamber of Commerce
P.O. Box 412
Tomahawk, WI 54487
(715) 453-5334

Comments   The Hiawatha Trail was built and is operated by Lincoln
County. It follows the abandoned Milwaukee Road railroad
bed and goes north from Tomahawk to the Lincoln County
line near Lake Nokomis, approximately 6.6 miles.

Eventually, it will join with the Bearskin Trail to the north.
The trail is surfaced with screened rotten granite, and is
frequented by hikers. There is no admission charge, and
there are numerous private campgrounds, hotels, and resorts
in the area.

P Parking	**👫** Restrooms
🏠 Shelter	**?** Information
▬▬▬▬▬▬▬▬▬	Mtn. Biking
= = = = = = = = = = = =	Hiking
▬▬▬▬▬▬▬▬▬	Roadway

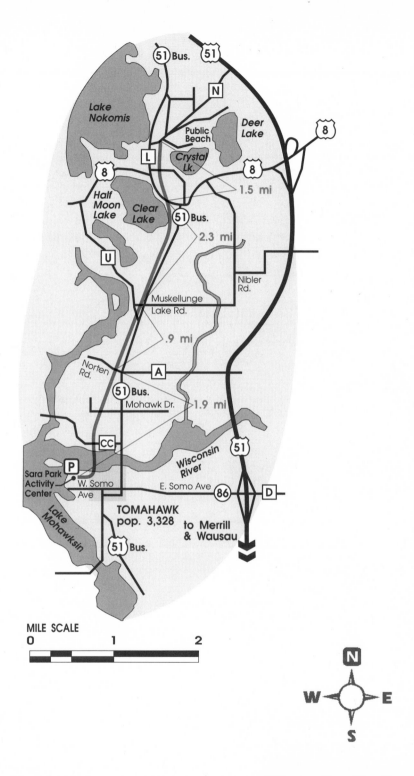

Hiawatha Trail

Lumberjack Trail

Trail Length   12 miles

Effort Level   Easy to moderate

Setting   Gently rolling, heavily wooded.

Location   From Boulder Junction, south 1 mile on old Hwy. K to Concora Road; or approximately 6 miles southeast of Boulder Junction on County Hwy. K to the east side of White Sand Lake.

Information   Wisconsin Dept. of Natural Resources
8779 Hwy. J
Woodruff, WI 54568
(715) 356-5211

Comments   The Lumberjack Trail winds along the edge of the Manitowish River, the Fishtrap Flowage, and the eastern end of White Sand Lake. The terrain is gently rolling with a variety of timber types. The trail is well marked with white and blue symbols, and there are mapboards located at intersections.

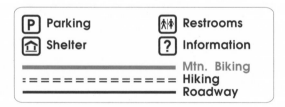

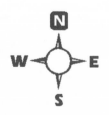

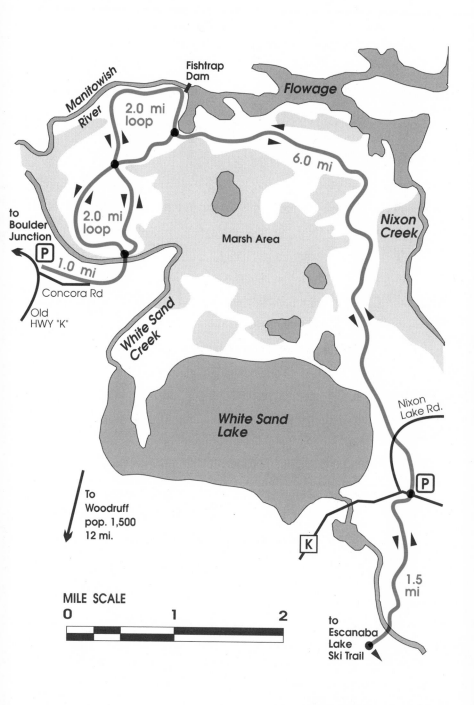

Manitowish River

Fishtrap Dam

Flowage

2.0 mi loop

6.0 mi

Nixon Creek

2.0 mi loop

to Boulder Junction

P

1.0 mi

Concora Rd

Old HWY "K"

Marsh Area

White Sand Creek

White Sand Lake

Nixon Lake Rd.

P

To Woodruff pop. 1,500 12 mi.

K

1.5 mi

MILE SCALE

0   1   2

to Escanaba Lake Ski Trail

Lumberjack Trail

67

Madeline Lake Trail

Trail Length	9.5 miles
Effort Level	Easy to moderate
Setting	Level to rolling terrain.
Location	2 miles southeast of Woodruff. Take Hwy. 51 to Hwy. J. East on Hwy. J to Rudolph Road and then north to trail.
Information	Wisconsin Dept. of Natural Resources 8779 Hwy. J Woodruff, WI 54568 (715) 356-5211
Comments:	The Madeline Lake Trail offers gently to rolling terrain, with a fair amount of level trail. Most of the trail follows old logging roads. The trail is well marked with white and blue symbols, and there are mapboards located at intersections. There is a shelter midway with a fire pit.

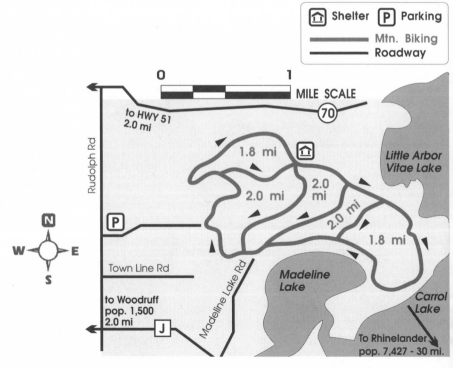

McNaughton Lake Trails

Trail Length   7.0 miles

Effort Level   Easy

Setting   Gentle terrain with a few steep hills. Mowed grass and dirt.

Location   13 miles south of Woodruff. Take Hwy. 47 east, through Lake Tomahawk. Turn right on Kildare Road.

Information   Wisconsin Dept. of Natural Resources
8779 Hwy. J
Woodruff, WI 54568
(715) 356-5211

Comments   The McNaughton Lake Trails mostly follow old logging roads. The terrain is gentle with very few steep hills. The surface is mowed grass and dirt and passes 3 different lakes. The trail is well marked with white and blue symbols. There are mapboards located at intersections. There is a shelter midway with a fire pit.

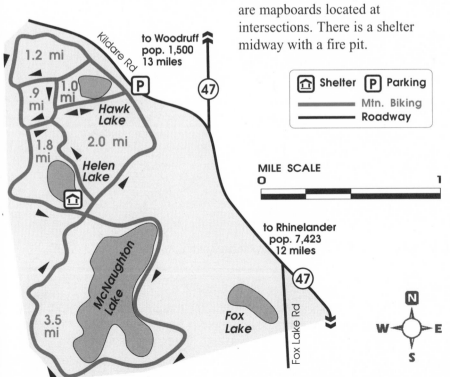

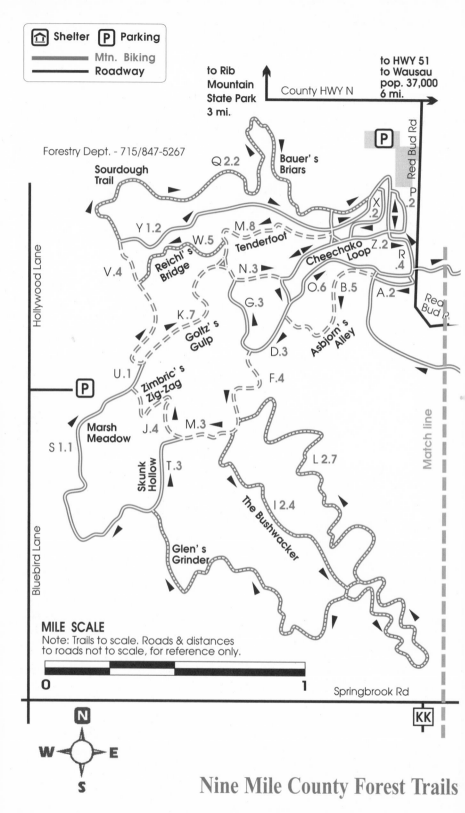

Nine Mile County Forest Trails

Nine Mile County Forest Trails

Trail Length   18.5 miles biking (30 miles total)

Effort Level   Easy to difficult

Setting   Wooded uplands, marshes, water impoundments.

Location   From Wausau at Hwy. 51 take Hwy N west approximately 3.5 miles to Red Bud Road, and then south 1.5 miles.

Information   Marathon County Forestry Dept.
500 Forest St.
Wausau, WI 54403
(715) 847-5267

Comments   Nine-Mile County Forest offers 4,755 acres of uplands, marshes, and water impoundments. The forest was named after Nine-Mile Swamp, a unique natural feature. Nine-Mile Forest has a well maintained system of trails and is known for its mountain biking, cross-country skiing, hiking, nature study, photography, berry picking and snowmobiling. Black Creek and Four-Mile Creek wind through open marsh, clumps of spruce and Nine-Mile Swamp.

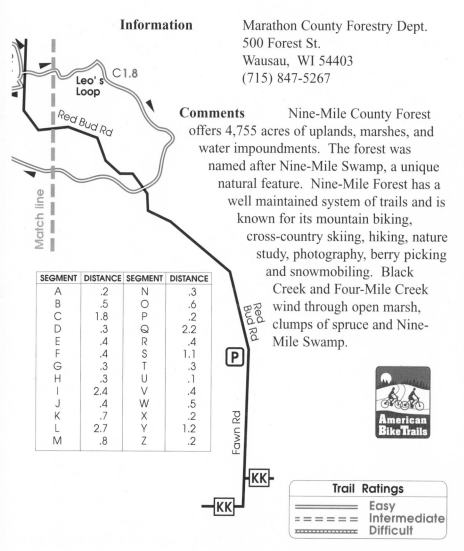

SEGMENT	DISTANCE	SEGMENT	DISTANCE
A	.2	N	.3
B	.5	O	.6
C	1.8	P	.2
D	.3	Q	2.2
E	.4	R	.4
F	.4	S	1.1
G	.3	T	.3
H	.3	U	.1
I	2.4	V	.4
J	.4	W	.5
K	.7	X	.2
L	2.7	Y	1.2
M	.8	Z	.2

Trail Ratings

Easy
Intermediate
Difficult

Shannon Lake Trail

Trail Length   7.6 miles

Effort Level   Easy to moderate

Setting   Gently rolling. Wooded.

Location   2.5 miles northeast of St. Germain. Take Hwy. 155 to Found
Lake Road. Another access is approximately 10 miles from
Eagle River on Hwy. G.

Information   Wisconsin Dept. of Natural Resources
8779 Hwy. J.
Woodruff, WI 54568
(715) 356-5211

Comments   The Shannon Lake Trails are gently rolling with a variety of
timber types. The trail is well marked with white and blue
symbols. There are mapboards located at intersections.

MILE SCALE

0   1

G

.5 mi

P to
Eagle River
pop.1.374
10 miles

2.7 mi

1.1 mi

.6 mi

Marsh Area

🏠 Shelter   P Parking
——— Mtn. Biking
——— Roadway

P

.4 mi

1.9 mi
loop

Found Lake Rd.

N

to
St. Germain
2.5 miles

Shannon
Lake

W ◆ E

Hill
Danger

S

Found
Lake

Beaver
Lake

Chequamegon National Forest

Taylor and Price County Area

Trail Lengths	Jaycee	15 miles
	Timm's Hill	10 miles
	Forest roads	100+ miles

Effort Level   Moderate

Setting   Forest, natural & groomed, roads

Location   Taylor and Price County are located in north central Wisconsin, northwest of Wausau and northeast of Eau Claire.

Information   Chequamegon National Forest
1170 4th Ave. S.
Park Falls, WI 54522

Price County Recreation Dept.
Normal Bldg.
Phillips, WI 54555

Comments   Try the very scenic, low usage, gravel forest roads in Chequamegon Forest. They also provide access to many unmarked logging trails in the area. The Jaycee & Timm's Hill Trails are recommended for Mountain Biking.

see map on next page

The Timm's Hill County Park

The Timm's Hill County Park is maintained by Price County at Timm's Hill. It features Wisconsin's highest natural point, a glacial hill, 1,951 feet above sea level. An excellent system of improved mountain biking and ski trails run through and around the park. Groomed for both diagonal and skate skiing. The trail surface is unmowed grassy surface.

The Rib Lake Trail System

The Rib Lake Trail System is mowed and well marked; the Ice Age Trail with yellow blazes, the Jaycee Trail with green blazes and the Timm's Hill National Trail with red blazes. Biking difficulty is moderate.

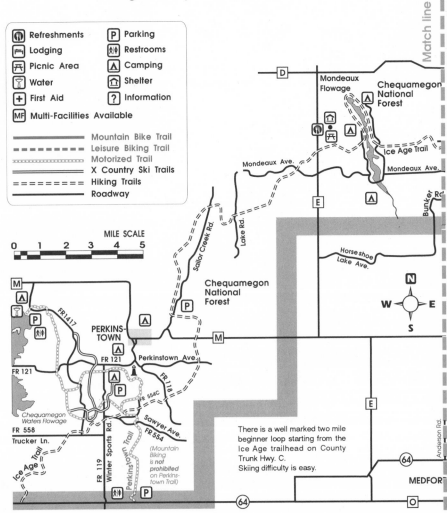

74

The Jaycee Trail

The Jaycee Trail is a 12 mile loop supplementing and interconnecting with the Ice Age National Scenic Trail north of Rib Lake. It is a mowed grass surface well maintained for skate and diagonal skiing. Biking and skiing difficulty is moderate. Marked by conspicuous green blazes.

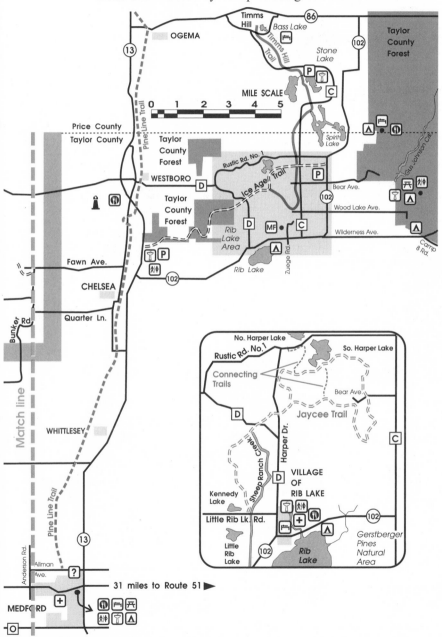

31 miles to Route 51 ▶

Chequamegon National Forest-Taylor and Price County Area

75

NORTH WEST
Mountain Biking Trails

section

6

Black Lake Trail 78

Governor Knowles State Forest 79

Brule River State Forest.. 80

Copper Falls State Park 82

Flambeau River State Forest.. 84

Tuscobia-Park Falls State Trail 86

Rock Lake Trail 88

Wintergreen Trail 89

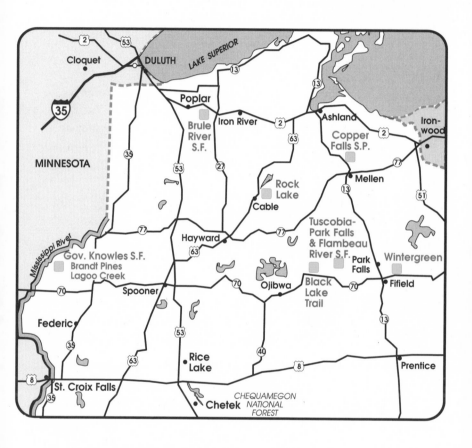

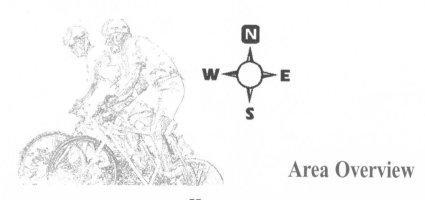

Area Overview

Black Lake Trail

Trail Length   4.0 miles

Effort Level   Easy

Setting   The trail circles Black Lake. The area was heavily lumbered during the early 1900's. Part of the trail follows an old logging road.

Location   From Hayward, 26 east on Hwy. B. At the Hwy. B and W intersection, turn left (north) on Fishtrap Road for 4.8 miles to FR 172. Continue (north) 3.3 miles on FR 172 to FR 173. Left on FR 173 for .5 miles to the FR 1666 (campground road). Turn right (east) on the blacktop road for .5 miles to a parking lot on the left (west) side of the road, which is also the trailhead.

Information   Hayward Ranger District
Rt. 10 Box 508
Hayward, WI 54843
(715) 634-4821

Comments   The trail is mostly a narrow path through the woods, and is nearly always in sight of Black Lake. There are 9 interpretive stops along the trail indicated by numbered posts. The area is noted for its pine and hemlock hardwood. Black Lake is a flowage on Fishtrap Creek.

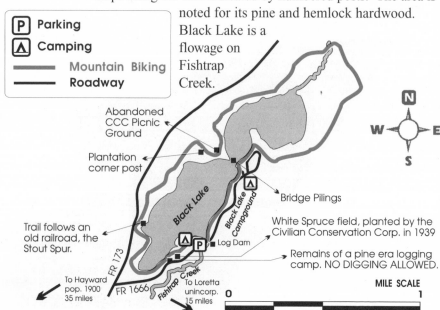

Governor Knowles
State Forest

Information   Governor Knowles State Forest
Hwy. 70, P.O. Box 367
Grantsburg, WI 54840
(715) 463-2898

Comments

The Forest borders the east side of the St. Croix River and is 55 miles long commencing at Hwy. 77 to the north.

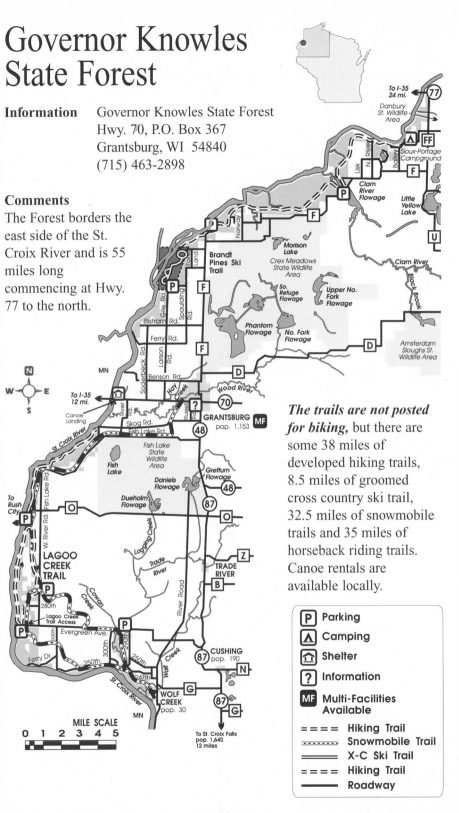

The trails are not posted for biking, but there are some 38 miles of developed hiking trails, 8.5 miles of groomed cross country ski trail, 32.5 miles of snowmobile trails and 35 miles of horseback riding trails. Canoe rentals are available locally.

P	Parking
A	Camping
⌂	Shelter
?	Information
MF	Multi-Facilities Available
====	Hiking Trail
········	Snowmobile Trail
——	X-C Ski Trail
====	Hiking Trail
▬▬	Roadway

MILE SCALE
0 1 2 3 4 5

Brule River State Forest

Trail Length   6.0 miles

Effort Level   Easy to Moderate

Setting   Rolling hills, deep forests.

Location   2 miles northwest of Brule on Hwy. 2, then west to trailhead and parking.

Information   Brule River State Forest
P.O. Box 125
Brule, WI 54820
(715) 372-4866

Comments   The After Hours Ski Trail in the Brule River State Forest offers a variety of terrain and forest. 'Main Street', the backbone of the trail, is relatively level while the Pine Loop provides a challenging hill through the pines. There is parking on the left side of After Hours Road. Take the far right trail past the gate. In addition, there are 15 miles of undesignated/unmarked trails and logging roads that are not posted against bicycle use.

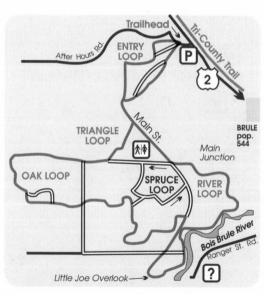

After Hours Ski Trail
from opposite page

	Miles	Effort Level
Entry Loop	1.0	Easy
Parking to Main Junction	1.0	Easy
Spruce Loop	1.0	Easy
River Loop	2.0	Moderate
Oak Loop	3.0	Moderate

0   1

MILE SCALE

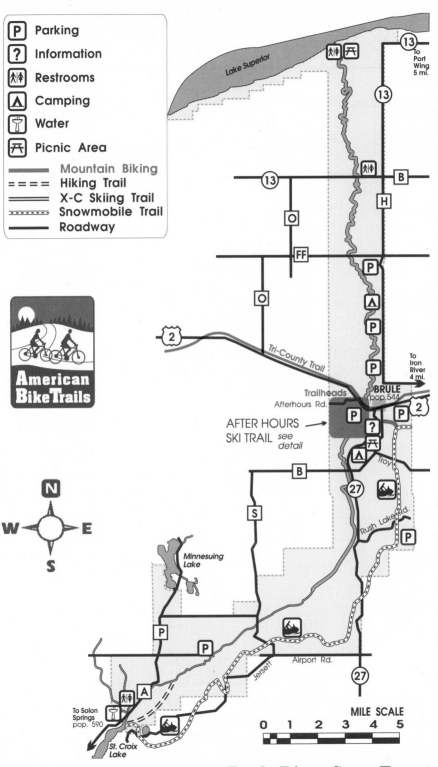

Legend:

- P Parking
- ? Information
- 🚹🚺 Restrooms
- ⚠ Camping
- 🚰 Water
- 🏕 Picnic Area

- Mountain Biking
- ==== Hiking Trail
- X-C Skiing Trail
- ········ Snowmobile Trail
- Roadway

American Bike Trails

Lake Superior

To Port Wing 5 mi.

To Iron River 4 mi.

Tri-County Trail

BRULE pop.544

Trailheads
Afterhours Rd.

AFTER HOURS SKI TRAIL *see detail*

Troy

Rush Lake Rd.

Minnesuing Lake

Airport Rd.

Jersett

To Solon Springs pop. 590

St. Croix Lake

N
W E
S

MILE SCALE

0 1 2 3 4 5

Brule River State Forest

Copper Falls State Park

Trail Length   8.3 miles

Effort Level   Easy to difficult

Setting   Rolling terrain, hilly.

Location   2 miles north to Mellen on Hwy. 169, then 2 miles on Hwy. J. The trailhead is west of the main park entrance road about .3 miles from the park office and shortly after the ball fields. Take the right trail split.

Information   Copper Falls State Park
R.R. 1, Box 17AA
Mellen, WI 54546
(715) 463-2898

Comments: The Park is named for the 29 foot falls that is the beginning of the Bad River as it flows through some two miles of steeped-walled canyons of rugged splendor. The walls of the gorge rise 60 to 100 feet. The falls, river and rock walls become a breathtaking experience. Don't pass it up. Close to Copper Falls is a picnic area and a concession stand. In addition to biking, there are 14 miles (6 loops) of cross-country ski trails, and 7 miles of hiking trails including a self-guided nature trail.

?	Information	P	Parking
⌂	Shelter	👥	Restrooms
🔧	Bicycle Service	A	Camping
🚰	Drinking Fountain	🎋	Picnic Area

━━━━━━━━━ Mountain Biking
= = = = = = = = = Hiking Trail
━━━━━━━━━ X-C Skiing Trail
················· Snowmobile Trail
━━━━━━━━━ Roadway

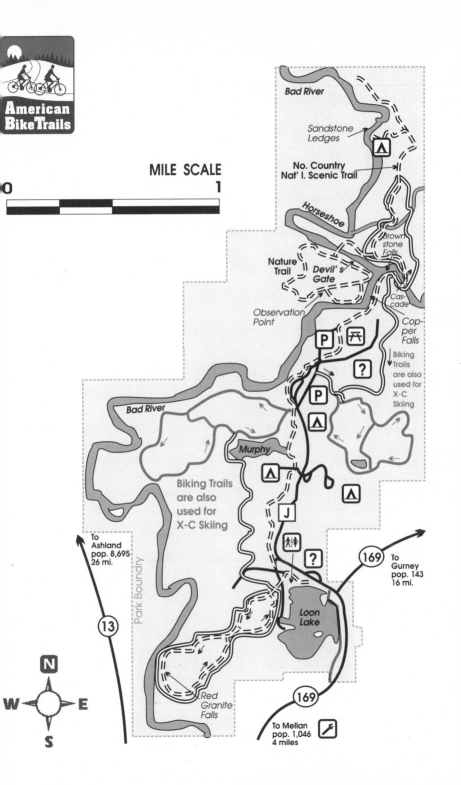

Copper Falls State Park

Flambeau River State Forest

Trail Length   Over 100 miles

Effort Level   Easy to difficult

Setting   Forests

Location   Approximately 10 miles southwest of Park Falls between Hwy. 70 to the north and Hwy. 8 to the south.

Information   Flambeau River State Forest
1613 County Rd. W
Winter, WI 54896
(715) 332-5271

Comments   The trail between Hwy. W and Hwy. 70 provides 14 miles of easy to difficult marked trail for biking or hiking. The trail is wide and very hilly, making for an exciting mountain bike trip.

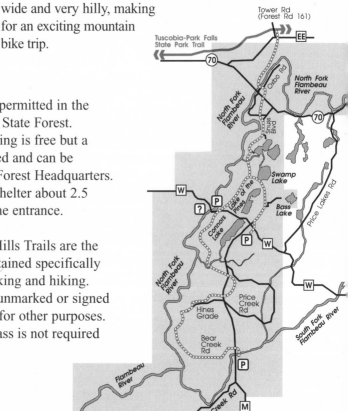

Backpacking is permitted in the Flambeau River State Forest. Overnight camping is free but a permit is required and can be obtained at the Forest Headquarters. There is a trail shelter about 2.5 miles north of the entrance.

The Flambeau Hills Trails are the only trails maintained specifically for mountain biking and hiking. Other trails are unmarked or signed and maintained for other purposes. The state trail pass is not required on these trails.

Oxbo Trails

Loop 1	easy, 2.4 miles
Loop 2	easy, 1.2 miles
Loop 3	moderate, 2.4 miles
Loop 4	moderate, .6 miles
Loop 5	moderate, 1.2 miles

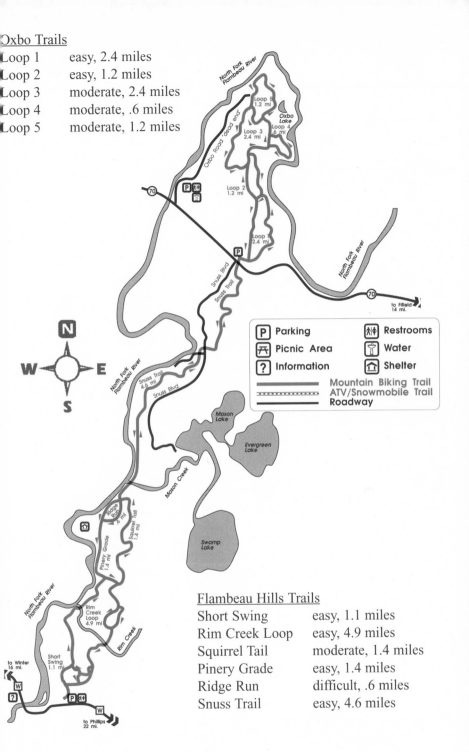

Flambeau Hills Trails

Short Swing	easy, 1.1 miles
Rim Creek Loop	easy, 4.9 miles
Squirrel Tail	moderate, 1.4 miles
Pinery Grade	easy, 1.4 miles
Ridge Run	difficult, .6 miles
Snuss Trail	easy, 4.6 miles

Flambeau River State Forest

Tuscobia-Park Falls State Trail

Trail Length   74 miles

Effort Level   Easy

Setting   The trail is an abandoned railroad grade, with loose gravel and cinders. Open areas, lightly wooded, small communities.

Location   The trail runs from Park Falls at the eastern trailhead to Tuscobia, a few miles north of Rice Lake, at the western trailhead.

Information   Tuscobia Trail DNR
P.O. Box 187
Winter, WI 54896
(715) 634-6513

PARK FALLS EAST TRAILHEAD

Access trailhead by turning west off HWY 13 at Division Street and proceed 5 blocks to 9th Avenue. Trail is 1 block south of Division Street.

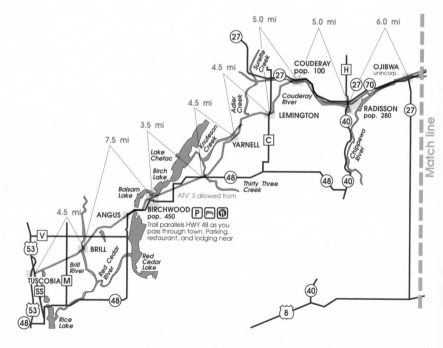

TUSCOBIA-PARK FALLS STATE TRAIL ROUTE SLIP:

Park Falls	SEGMENT	TOTAL
Kaiser Rd.	3.5	3.5
Log Creek	9.0	12.5
Draper	6.0	18.5
Loretta	1.0	19.5
Winter (HWY W)	9.0	28.5
Ojibwa	5.0	33.5
Radisson	6.0	39.5
Couderay	5.0	44.5
Lemington (HWY C)	5.0	49.5
Yarnell Rd. (N/S)	4.5	54.0
HWY 48 (E/W)	4.5	58.5
Birchwood	3.5	62.0
Brill (27th Ave.)	7.5	69.5
HWY 53	4.5	74.0

WEST TRAILHEAD

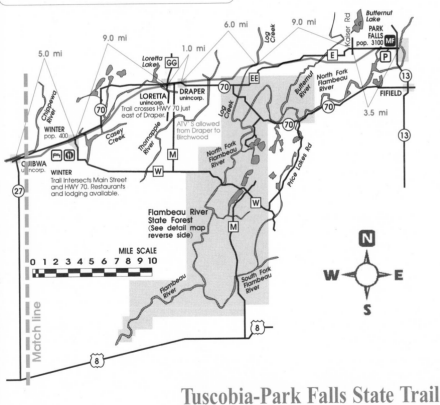

BRILL

RICE LAKE
pop. 8,000

Access trailhead by exiting HWY 53 at HWY 48. Proceed east to HWY SS and then north. Trailhead begins off HWY SS just before it passes under HWY 53. The Country Inn restaurant is 1/4 mile south.

P Parking	**⊞** Picnic Area
🛏 Lodging	**⊕** Refreshments
? Information	**MF** Multi-Facility
══════ Mtn. Biking Trail	
────── Roadway	

Tuscobia-Park Falls State Trail

Rock Lake Trail

Trail Length	25 miles (loops)
Effort Level	Easy to difficult
Setting	Rolling terrain, hills, forested, ridges
Location	7.5 miles east of Cable and 12 miles west of Clam Lake on Hwy. M.
Information	Hayward District Ranger Chequamegon National Forest Rt. 10, Box 508 Hayward, WI 54843 (715) 634-4821
Comments	Mountain biking is popular. Much of the trail parallels old logging roads, which have fewer hills but are not as smooth as the trails for those who find climbing the hills on the trail too challenging.

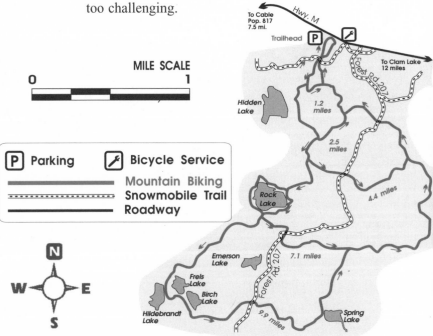

Wintergreen Trail

Trail Length   15.4 miles

Effort Level   Moderate to difficult

Setting   Forests. Upland ridges to lowland marshes.

Location   5 miles east of Fifield and north of Hwy. 70. Fifield is 4 miles south of Park Falls at Hwy 70 and 13.

Information   Forest Technician
Chequamegon National Forest
1170 4th Ave. South
Park Falls, WI 54552
(715) 762-2461

P	Parking
木木	Restrooms
🎪	Picnic Area
▬▬▬	Mountain Biking
•••••••	Snowmobile Trail
▬▬▬	Roadway

Comments   The trail offers a variety of routes through rolling terrain, ranging from upland ridges to lowland marshes. There are scenic vistas overlooking several ponds and bogs. The trail passes through a mixture of forest from lowland conifers and red pine, to northern hardwoods and young aspen.There are parking and toilet facilities at the trailhead.

Wet Swampy Area

LOOP C - 2.2 mi.

LOOP B 3.2 mi.

LOOP D 2 mi.

.8 mi.

1 mi.

1 mi.

Luder Rd.

LOOP A 1.3

.7 mi.

.4 mi.

SHORT-CUT

KIDDIE TRAIL

.8 mi.

FR 549

MILE SCALE

0   1

To Park Falls pop. 3,100

P

70

13   To Fifield pop. 863 5 miles

木木

Trailhead

Riding Tips

- In Wisconsin, the wind is usually out of the southwest. Consider riding west in the early morning when the wind is calm, and then east in the afternoon with the wind at your back.

- Pushing in gears that are too high can push knees beyond their limits. Avoid extremes by pedaling faster rather than shifting into a higher gear.

- Keeping your elbows bent, changing your hand position frequently and wearing bicycle gloves all help to reduce the numbness or pain in the palm of the hand from long-distance riding.

- Keep you pedal rpms up on an uphill so you have reserve power if you lose speed.

- Stay in a high-gear on a level surface, placing pressure on the pedals and resting on the handle bars and saddle.

- Lower your center of gravity on a long or steep downhill run by using the quick release seat post binder and dropping the saddle height down.

- Rocking the bike gives you more efficient pumping. This means pulling up on the left hand grip as you push down the left pedal and vice versa.

- Brake intermittently on a rough surface.

- Complete your braking process before bumping over sizable objects.

- If your wheel drops into a deep rut, brake to a stop immediately. If you try to climb out, the front wheel will jam.

- When riding over thick sticks or branches, make sure to cross them close to their mid-sections. Hitting one near its end can flip it up into your spokes.

- Never start biking on unfamiliar trails late in the day and always carry a compass.

- Cross-country trail systems used for biking are commonly marked in kilometers, which is roughly two thirds of a mile.

Camba Trails

The CAMBA trails lie in and around the beautiful Chequamegon National Forest as well as in Bayfield and Sawyer County Forests— nearly a million acres in which to ride your fat tire bike. Of this, CAMBA has adopted an area of approximately 1,600 square miles. The system is divided into six clusters, each with one or more trail heads. The following pages provide an overview of the entire system together with more detailed maps of each cluster.

CAMBA's user-friendly system is designed to encourage off-road bicyclists to enjoy and explore the Chequamegon area. Trail markings include frequent reassurance markers, intersection *"You Are Here"* markers with a corresponding land marker number on the map, and a sign board with an overview map and map dispenser at each trail head.

Each CAMBA cluster is comprised of 25 to 75 miles of trail. Trail Clusters are located near the communities of Cable, Delta, Drummond, Hayward, Namakagon and Seeley.

The routes follow a variety of paths, including logging roads, fire lanes, snowmobile trails, ski trails and single track. The terrain lends itself to riders of all abilities, from beginners to seasoned fat tire experts. There are no paved bike paths in the system.

As you explore the CAMBA system, you'll ride through rolling terrain dotted with lakes, rivers, streams, ridges and meadows carved by glaciers during the last ice age. The entire system is heavily wooded and wildlife is plentiful. Wildflowers bloom from late May through the summer. From June through September, berry picking can add a tasty diversion to your tour. The fall colors begin in late August and reach their splendid peak near the end of September. Most trails in the system are ridable from April through November.

Several area bike shops offer rentals, repairs and trail riding recommendations, as well as bike sales, clothing and accessories. Northwest Wisconsin is an outdoor recreation paradise — home of the American Birkebeiner, Chequamegon Fat Tire Festival, and the Firehouse 50—and an area which welcomes off-road cyclists with open arms. For lodging assistance and other information, call (800)533-7454.

Camba Clusters
Mountain Biking Trails

section

7

Delta Cluster 94

Drummond Cluster 96

Cable Cluster 98

Seeley Cluster 100

Hayward Cluster 102

Namakagon Cluster 104

Chequamegon Area Mountain Bike Association

Welcome to the adventure of mountain biking in northwest Wisconsin

The **CAMBA** Off-road Bike Trail System consists of over 200 miles of marked and mapped routes through a wilderness of striking beauty and peaceful solitude. Area cyclists have created the CAMBA system to make this vast, unique area available to everyone.

CAMBA is a nonprofit association dedicated to the development and promotion of mountain biking opportunities in the Chequamegon National Forest area of northwest Wisconsin.

For a complete set of maps of the entire CAMBA system including five individual cluster maps suitable for navigation, send $5.00 to:

CAMBA
P.O. Box 141
Cable, WI 54821

For membership information, call (800) 533-7454.

BBS   (715) 798-4580

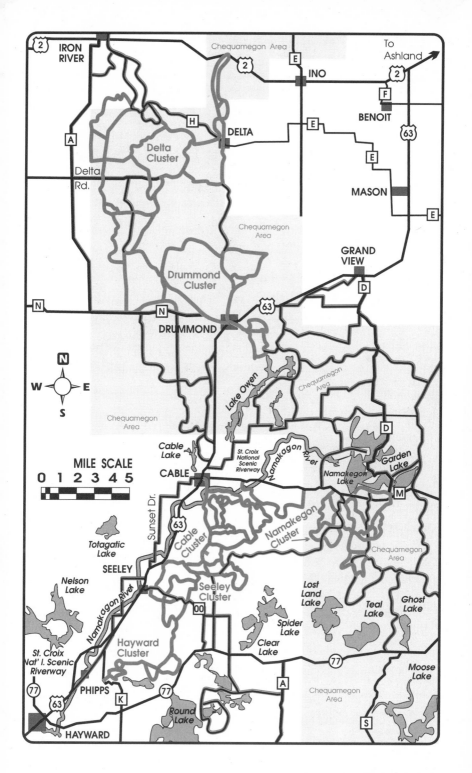

Area Overview

Delta Cluster

Trail Length
East Fork Loop	11.0 mi.
South Fork Loop	8.7 mi.
Pine Barrens Loop	8.4 mi.
Tall Pines Loop	12.4 mi.
West Fork Loop	14.0 mi.
Buckskin Loop	10.8 mi.

Effort Level Easy to difficult single track sections

Location

<u>Delta Lake Park Trail Head</u>

From Drummond, go north on Delta-Drummond Rd. (FH35) for 10 miles to Hwy. H. Left (west) on Hwy. H for 1/4 mile, and then left (west) on Scenic Drive for 1 1/4 miles to Delta Lake County Park. The parking lot is on the right.

<u>Twin Bear Lake Park Trail Head</u>

From Iron River 6 miles southeast on Hwy. H. turn left into the Bayfield County Twin Bear Lake Park where the trailhead is located.

<u>Wanoka Trailhead</u>

From Iron River east on Hwy. 2 for 7.6 miles, and then right (south) on FR 234 for .7 miles to the Trail Head.

<u>Tall Pines Trail Head</u>

From Drummond drive west on Hwy. N for 5.8 miles, and then right (north) on Beck Road (FR 229) for 5.5 miles to the Trail Head.

Comments The trail surfaces feature light, but fine soils suitable for all weather riding. All trails form a series of interconnecting loops and it is also possible to connect with the Drummond Cluster to the south. Delta Cluster's moderate trails offer the best variety in riding by including all the available road and trail types. The easiest trails follow paved and improved gravel or dirt forest roads. They are the South Fork Loop and the East Fork's Barren's Cutoff Loop. The Tall Pines and the Buckskin Loops are almost entirely off-road. The Delta Loop is the most challenging trail, offering scenic but consistently hilly terrain.

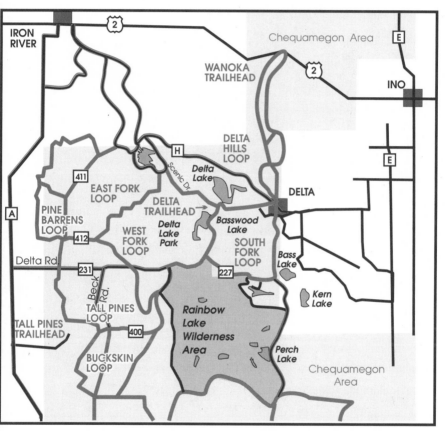

IRON RIVER

Chequamegon Area

WANOKA TRAILHEAD

DELTA HILLS LOOP

DELTA

Delta Lake

EAST FORK LOOP

DELTA TRAILHEAD

PINE BARRENS LOOP

WEST FORK LOOP

Delta Lake Park

Basswood Lake

SOUTH FORK LOOP

Bass Lake

Delta Rd.

Kern Lake

Beck Rd.

TALL PINES LOOP

Rainbow Lake Wilderness Area

TALL PINES TRAILHEAD

Perch Lake

Chequamegon Area

BUCKSKIN LOOP

Mountain Biking Trail
Roadway

MILE SCALE

0 1 2 3 4 5

Delta Cluster

Drummond Cluster

Effort Level   Easy to moderate - road sections & ski trails

Length & Description

Horse Pasture Loop	18.2 miles; dirt roads, double track, asphalt
Pigeon Lake Loop	11.4 miles; dirt road, double track, asphalt
Star Lake Loop	11.6 miles; dirt road, double track, asphalt
Cisco Lake Loop	4.6 miles; dirt road, double track asphalt
Reynard Lake Loop	14.8 miles; dirt roads, single & double track, asphalt
Boulevard Loop	9.3 miles; asphalt, dirt road, double & single track
Jack Rabbit Loop	6.7 miles; asphalt, dirt road, double track
Antler Loop	5.4 miles; asphalt, dirt road, double & single track

Comments   The Drummond Cluster provides mostly beginning to intermediate grade loop for the cyclist who wants to get into the woods, but may not be comfortable with a great deal of single track riding through the deep woods. All loops starting at the Drummond Town Park Trail Head have a majority of gentle forest road riding and some pavement. The terrain is level to gently rolling. These loops present good all season riding. You can also access the Delta Cluster to the north.

The balance of the Drummond Cluster trails originate from the Drummond Ski Trails Trail Head. They are all woods roads, double track or easy single track. With only a few good hills, these trails are a good choice for someone wanting to experience single track with a deep woods feel, but without committing to a long distance technical ride. The Boulevard Loop has the added attraction of a destination stop at beautiful Lake Owen where you can picnic and swim.

Drummond Cluster

Easy road sections & a moderate ski trail. Accesses the
Flynn & Star Lakes non-motorized areas.

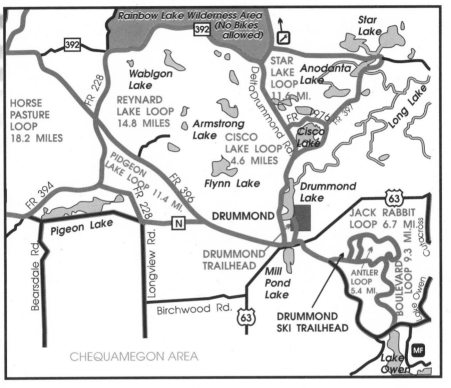

To Trailhead:

From Hwy. 63, turn left (N) on Wisc. St. at
the Black Bear. Go 3 blocks & turn left
(W) at the T intersection on Superior St. to
the town park in Drummond.

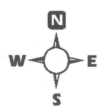

Drummond Cluster

Cable Cluster

Effort Level   Easy to difficult

Length & Description

<u>Trails Beginning at Cable Trail Head</u>

Short & Fat	15.1 miles from Cable to Telemark trailheads
	18.5 mile loop with return via McNaught Road: gravel/rock/sand road, grassy ski trail, some pavement.

Short & Fat Cutoffs	Power Line Cutoff	5.5 miles
	Timber Trail Cutoff	11 miles
	Telemark Springs Cutoff	9.6 miles

<u>Loop Trails Beginning at Telemark Resort</u>

Nature Trail	3.8 mile loop; narrow single track grassy, Birkie trail
Sleigh Trail	9.5 mile loop; single & double track, Birkie trail
Esker Trail	6.7 mile loop; hilly single track, dirt road, some pavement
Spring Creek Trail	10.2 mile loop; gravel/sand town road, some pavement

Comments   The Chequamegon Fat Tire Festival 15.1 miles Short and Fat race course has been permanently marked as part of the CAMBA system. The Short & Fat criss-crosses and then joins the American Birkebeiner Trail until its conclusion at Telemark Resort. Other Cable Cluster Trails include those originating at Telemark Resort Trail Head. The most challenging is the Esker Trail, which climbs and dives and climbs again before finally beginning to climb the rocky glacial esker for which it is named. The trail continues to traverse densely wooded and rolling terrain until it finally breaks from the woods into steeply rolling, wide open grassy hills. For easy to moderate single and double track riding, try the Nature Trail or Sleigh Trail, both also originating from Telemark Resort. The Cable Cluster connects easily to the Seeley Cluster to the south.

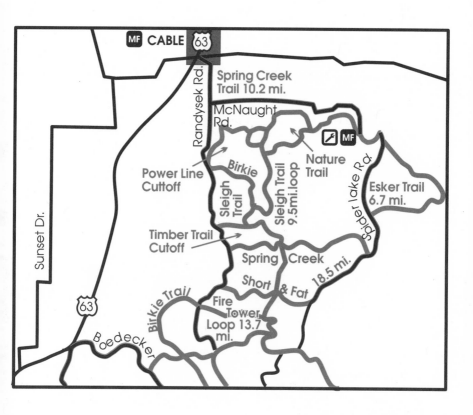

MILE SCALE

0 1 2 3 4

Bicycle Service   **MF** Multi-Facilities Available

Mountain Biking Trail
Snowmobile Trail
Roadway

N
W   E
S

Cable Cluster

Seeley Cluster

<u>Loops begin at road 00 and Silverthorn Park Trail Head</u>

Effort Level   Moderate to Difficult

Length & Description

Winding Pine Loop	8.5 miles, double track, gravel, dirt, paved road. Gradual climbs and rocky descents.
Fire Tower Loop	13.7 miles, double track, gravel, dirt, paved road. Gradual climbs and rocky descents.
Lake Helane Loop	14.5 miles, double track, gravel, dirt, paved road. Gradual climbs and rocky descents.
Frost Pocket Loop	6.7 miles from 00 trailhead, 9.7 miles from Silverthorn trailhead. Dirt road, double track, asphalt
Northern Lights Loop	5.2 miles, easy, gravel, asphalt, grassy, single track.
Birkie Trail	12 miles one way Boedecker Road to Power Line. Grass and single track. 9 miles one way Mosquito Brook to 00. Grass and single track.
Phipps Fire Lane	7.7 miles one way from Phipps to 00. Dirt Road.

Comments   The three Seeley Cluster loops north of County Highway 00 traverse the Seeley Hills about the Namakagon River Valley. Each of the three trails brings you through beautiful pine, birch, and hardwood forests. The three interconnecting loops are fairly well traveled double track gravel to dirt to grassy descents. The Seeley Cluster connects easily to the Hayward Cluster to the south and Cable Cluster to the north.

Interesting riding can also be found south of County Highway 00 in the Seeley area. The Frost Pocket Loop offers extremely varied riding for a seven mile loop. The frost pockets on Snowmobile Trail 8 are huge potholes once filled with buried chunks of ice left over from the glacier.

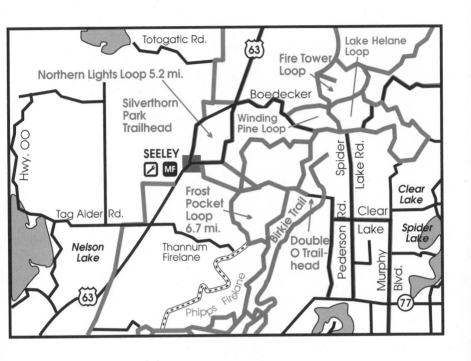

Totogatic Rd.

63

Fire Tower Loop

Lake Helane Loop

Northern Lights Loop 5.2 mi.

Boedecker

Silverthorn Park Trailhead

Winding Pine Loop

Hwy. OO

SEELEY

MF

Spider Lake Rd.

Clear Lake

Frost Pocket Loop 6.7 mi.

Birkie Trail

Clear Lake

Spider Lake

Tag Alder Rd.

Double O Trailhead

Pederson Rd.

Murphy Blvd.

Nelson Lake

Thannum Firelane

Phipps Firelane

63

77

MILE SCALE

0 1 2 3 4 5

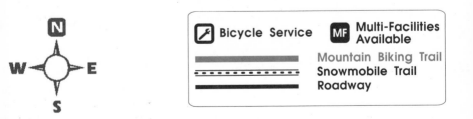

N

W — E

S

Bicycle Service

MF Multi-Facilities Available

Mountain Biking Trail
Snowmobile Trail
Roadway

Seeley Cluster

101

Hayward Cluster

Effort Level   Easy to moderate - roads & ski trails

<u>Trails begin at Mosquito Brook Trail Head</u>

Length and Description

Whitetail Loop	4.3 miles—Birkie trail, dirt roads, double track loop
Loop Descente	8.6 miles round trip (2.5 miles loop only)—Dirt road, double track, Birkie trail
Plantation Loop	9.2 miles round trip (2 miles loop only)—Dirt road, double track, Birkie trail
Bar Stool Loop	11.8 miles round trip (3.6 miles loop only)—Dirt roads, single & double track, Birkie trail

Comments   The Hayward Cluster features four loops, all are four miles long or less, and are easily accessed from the Mosquito Brook Trail Head. All four loops can be combined for a 13 mile ride. The loops feature short sections of the Birkie trail, as well as old rugged logging roads and single track that wind through hardwoods and pine plantations. From the outer most loop you can ride to the Phipps Fire Lane north to the "00" Trail Head. To return to the Mosquito Brook Trail Head, ride the Birkie Trail south, resulting in a varied loop of about 18 miles. The Cable Cluster connects easily to the Seeley Cluster to the south.

The ridges of the rolling hills on the east side of the Namekagon River valley between Hayward and Seeley are heavily forested. You will ride beneath a leafy canopy on most of the trails.

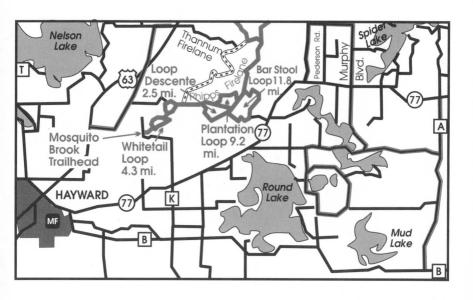

Nelson Lake

T

Thannum Firelane

63 US

Loop Descente 2.5 mi.

Phipps Firelane

Bar Stool Loop 11.8 mi.

Pederson Rd.

Murphy Blvd.

Spider Lake

77

A

Mosquito Brook Trailhead

Whitetail Loop 4.3 mi.

Plantation Loop 9.2 mi.

77

HAYWARD

77

K

MF

B

Round Lake

Mud Lake

B

Bicycle Service

MF Multi-Facilities Available

Mountain Biking Trail
Snowmobile Trail
Roadway

MILE SCALE

0 1 2 3 4 5

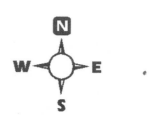

N
W E
S

Hayward Cluster

Namakagon Cluster

Namakagon Loop

Length	10 miles	
Effort Level	Moderate to difficult	
Description	Double & single tracks	

Rock Lake Loop

Length	9.9 miles	
Effort Level	Moderate to difficult	
Description	Double & single tracks	

Glacier Loop

Length	10 miles	
Effort Level	Moderate	
Description	Double & single tracks	

Patsy Lake Loop Trail

Length	12.5 miles	
Effort Level	Easy to moderate	
Description	Double & single tracks	

Comments   The Namakagon Cluster includes parts of the Rock Lake National Recreation Trails, all of which are suitable for off-road biking, but only the 16K (10 mile) ski trail is mapped and marked as part of the CAMBA system. The trails in this area are very challenging with a large percentage of single tracks. They take in some extraordinary beautiful wild scenery.

Just east of the Rock Lake Trails is an area of over 20 square miles of National Forest that contains three additional CAMBA trails. For moderately challenging 10 mile rides, try the Glacier or Namakagon Trails, originating at the Rock Lake and Namakagon Trail Heads respectively. Each trail in this cluster is comprised of an assortment of old logging roads, snowmobile trails or ski trails and cover an assortment of terrain and forest variety - from dense hardwood canopy to open aspen barrens to stands of old growth pine. Highlights include numerous wilderness lakes and views of lush open wet land areas.

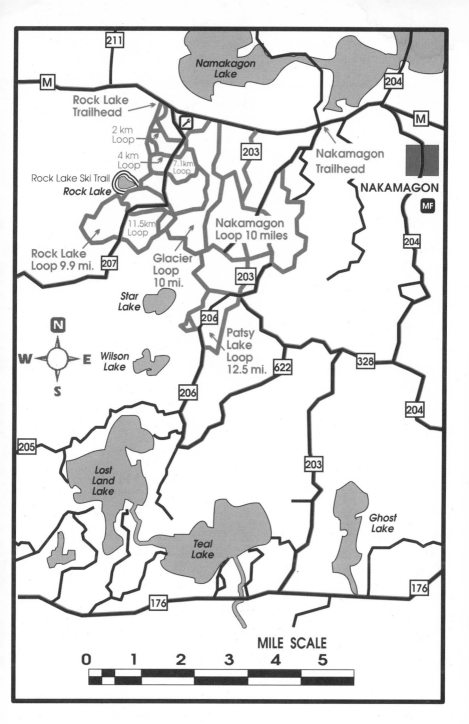

Namakagon Cluster

Canoeing in Wisconsin
An alternate adventure — Selected waterways convenient to trails

Black River State Forest Area

Black River—Canoeing is most popular along the central stretch. Hall's Creek Landing is 13.5 miles north of Black River Falls, from where the river flows through quiet forests to a landing above the dam at Black River Falls. From the canoe landing on First Street below the dam is a inviting 30-mile ride to New Amsterdam.

Brule River State Forest Area

Brule River—Medium to hazard rapids combined with smooth water, and navigable from its source at Solon Springs to its mouth on the Mississippi River. Common starting point is Stone's Bridge (Hwy. S). Upstream there are no rapids. The downstream trip can end at canoe landings near Hwy B or 2. Below Hwy 2 are dangerous rapids.

Flambeau River State Forest Area

Flambeau River—The north fork provides the most stable water flow. The upper sections are easier to canoe, while the southern section provide the challenge of rapids and whitewater. The most traveled stretch is from Nine Mile Creek to Ladysmith.

Hiawatha Trail Area

Tomahawk River—Medium to fast current including two difficult rapids on the lower stretches of the river. You can access at dams and road crossings.

Lake Wissota and Lowes Creek Area

Chippewa River—The river is navigable for most of its length to the Mississippi River. Water levels vary and should be checked locally. Access is available at road crossings.

Mirror Lake Area

Baraboo River—No rapids or falls, but a relaxing canoe outing. There are three dams requiring portage. Access is available at road crossings.

Oconto Area

Oconto River—There are 15 rated rapids along the northernmost section above Chute Pond (south of Mountain). Be sure to check water levels locally. The river below Chute Pond is moderate.

Wildcat Mountain State Park Area

Kickapoo River—Flows from north of Ontario to the Wisconsin River at Wauzeka. Entire length is navigable. A popular river with access at numerous road crossing. Current is relaxing. Rentals available.

Wyalusing State Park Area

Grant River—Frequent rapids. Winds through deep valleys bounded by rocky ledges and high bluffs. Numerous access points.

Wisconsin River—Flows 430 miles across the State to its junction with the Mississippi River at Wyalusing State Park. The southern 50 miles is especially popular with its beautiful scenery and numerous islands and no portaging. Canoe rentals available at many towns.

For additional information and brochures contact:

DNR Bureau of Parks and Recreation
P.O. Box 7921
Madison, WI   53707
Phone   608/266-2181.

Wisconsin Tourism Information

South East

Baraboo   Pop. 9,200
Chamber of Commerce
P.O. Box 442
Baraboo, WI 53913
(608)356-8333 or (800)BARABOO
Devil's Lake State Park

Burlington   Pop. 8,900
Chamber of Commerce
112 E. Chestnut St., Box 156
Burlington, WI 53913
(414)763-6044
Bong State Recreation Area

Elkhorn   Pop. 5,337
Walworth Cnty Tourism Council
P.O. Box 1015
Elkhorn, WI 53121
(414)723-3980 or (800)395-8687
Kettle Moraine SF - south unit

Oconomowoc   Pop. 11,000
Bureau of Tourism
174 E. Wisconsn Ave.
Oconomowoc, WI 53066
(414)569-2185 or (800)524-3744
Lapham Peak

Plymouth   Pop. 7,000
Chamber of Commerce
P.O. Box 584
Plymouth, WI 53073
(414)893-0079
Kettle Moraine State Forest-N Unit

Port Washington Pop. 10,000
Chamber of Commerce
P.O. Box 514
Port Washington, WI 53074
(414)284-0900
Harrington Beach State Park

Sheboygan   Pop. 104,000
Visitors Bureau
712 Riverfront St., Suite 101
Sheboygan, WI 53081
(414)457-9495
Kohler-Andrae State Park

Waukesha   Pop. 57,000
Area Tourism Council
223 Wisconsin Ave.
Waukesha, WI 53186
(414)542-0330 or (800)366-8474
Lapham Peak

Whitewater   Pop. 12,636
Chamber of Commerce
402 W. Main St., P.O. Box 34
Whitewater, WI 53190
(414)473-4005
Kettle Moraine SF-south unit

South West

Baraboo   Pop. 9,200
Chamber of Commerce
P.O. Box 442
Baraboo, WI 53913
(608)356-8333 or (800)BARABOO
Mirror Lake State Park

Dodgeville   Pop. 3,840
Chamber of Commerce
P.O. Box 141
Dodgeville, WI 53533
(608)935-5993
Governor Dodge State Park

North East

Elroy   Pop. 1,500
Advancement Corporation
1410 Academy St., P.O. Box 52
Elroy, WI 53929
(608)462-BIKE
Wildcat Mountain State Park

La Crosse   Pop. 51,000
Visitors Bureau
410 E. Veterans Memorial Dr.
La Crosse, WI 54602
(608)782-2366 or (800)658-9424
Perrot State Park

Mount Horeb   Pop. 4,182
Chamber of Commerce
P.O. Box 84
Mount Horeb, WI 53572
(608)437-5914
Blue Mound State Park

Prairie du Chien   Pop. 5,659
Tourism Council
211 S. Main St., P.O. Box 326
Prairie du Chien, WI 53821
(608)326-8555 or (800)PDC-1673
Wyalusing State Park

Trempealeau   Pop. 1,039
Chamber of Commerce
P.O. Box 212
Trempealeau, WI 54661
(608)534-6780
Perrot State Park

Appleton   Pop. 66,000
Fox Cities Visitors Bureau
110 Fox River Dr.
Appleton, WI 54915
(414)734-3358
High Cliff

Lakewood
Chamber of Commerce
P.O. Box 87
Lakewood, WI 54138
(715)276-6500
Oconto County Recreation Trail

Manitowoc   Pop. 35,520
Visitor Bureau
P.O. Box 966
Manitowoc, WI 54221
(414)683-4388
Point Beach State Park

Sturgeon Bay   Pop. 9,200
Infomation Center
P.O. Box 212
Sturgeon Bay, WI 54235
(414)743-3924
Newport Beach State Park
Peninsula State Park
Potawatomi State Park

Wisconsin Tourism Information (Continued)

West Central

Black River Falls   Pop. 3,500
Chamber of Commerce
336 N. Water St.
Black River Falls, WI 54615
(715)284-4658
Black River State Forest

Chippewa Falls   Pop. 13,000
Chamber of Commerce
811 N. Bridge St.
Chippewa Falls, WI 54729
(715)723-0331
Lake Wissota State Park

Eau Claire   Pop. 57,000
Visitors Bureau
2127 Bracket Ave.
Eau Claire, WI 54701
(715)831-2345 or (800)344-FUNN
Lake Wissota State Park
Lowes Creek County Park

North Central

Boulder Junction
Chamber of Commerce
Hwy M South, P.O. Box 286
Boulder Junction, WI 54512
(715)385-2400
Lumberjack Trail

Eagle River   Pop. 1,400
Chamber of Commerce
116 S. Railroad St., Box 218
Eagle River, WI 54521
(715)479-8575
Shannon Lake Trail

Medford   Pop. 4,500
Chamber of Commerce
Box 172
Medford, WI 54451
(715)748-4729 or (800)257-4729
Chequamegon National Forest
Jaycee Trail
Timms Hill Trail

Merrill   Pop. 9,860
Chamber of Commerce
720 E. Second St.
Merrill, WI 54452
(715)536-9474
Council Grounds State Park

Minocqua   Pop. 1,300
Chamber of Commerce
Hwy 51 & Front St., PO Box 1006W
Minocqua, WI 54548
(715)356-5266 or (800)44-NORTH
Madeline Lake Trail
McNaughton Lake Trail

Rhinelander   Pop. 8,000
Chamber of Commerce
135 S. Stevens St., P.O. Box 795
Rhinelander, WI 54501
(715)3627464 or (800)236-4386
McNaughton Lake Trail

Saint Germain   Pop. 1,500
Chamber of Commerce
Dept. DT, Box 155
Saint Germain, WI 54558
(715)542-3423 or (800)727-7203
Shannon Lake Trail

Tomahawk Pop. 3,500
Chamber of Commerce
208 N. 4th St., P.O. Box 412
Tomahawk, WI 54487
(715)453-5334 or (800)569-2160
Hiawatha Trail

Wausau Pop. 37,000
Visitors Council
300 Third St., P.O. Box 6190
Wausau, WI 54402
(715)845-6231 or (800)236-WSAU
Nine Mile Trail

North West

Ashland Pop. 8,700
Chamber of Commerce
320 4th Ave. W., P.O. Box 746
Ashland, WI 54806
(715)682-2500 or (800)284-9484
Brule River State Forest

Cable Pop. 2,000
Chamber of Commerce
P.O. Box 217
Cable, WI 54821
(715)798-3833 or (800)533-7454
Camba Trail Clusters
Rock Lake Trail

Hayward Pop. 1,900
Chamber of Commerce
101 W. 1st St., P.O. Box 726
Hayward, WI 54843
(715)634-8662 or (800)826-3474
Brule River State Forest
CAMBA Clusters

Grantsburg Pop. 1,200
Chamber of Commerce
416 S. Pine St.
Grantsburg, WI 54840
(715)463-2405
Flambeau River State Forest
Governor Knowles State Forest

Mellen Pop. 935
Chamber of Commerce
125 E. Bennett St., P.O. Box 793
Mellen, WI 54546
(715)274-2330
Copper Falls State Park

Park Falls Pop. 3,100
Chamber of Commerce
400 4th Ave. S., P.O. Box 246
Park Falls, WI 54552
(715)762-2703
Tuscobia-Park Falls State Trail
Wintergreen Ski & Hiking Area

Rice Lake Pop. 8,000
Tourism Commission
37 S. Main St.
Rice Lake, WI 54868
(715)234-2126 or (800)523-6318
Tuscobia-Park Falls State Trail

Saint Croix Falls Pop. 1,640
Polk County Information
710 Hwy 35 So.
Saint Croix Falls, WI 54024
(715)483-1410 or (800)222-7655
Governor Knowles State Forest

Superior Pop. 27,134
Tourist Information Center
305 Harbor View Pkwy.
Superior, WI 54880
(715)392-2773 or (800)942-5313
Brule River State Forest

Detail Trail Maps Available

Waterproof, Tear resistent, 2 color, 2 sides, 11 by 17 inches

Map#	Illinois		Basic Data
IL01	Fox River Trail	¤	40 mi., paved/screenings
IL02	Illinois Prairie Path	¤	46 mi., screenings
IL03	Great Western	¤	18 mi., screenings
	Virgil Gilman	¤	11 mi., paved
IL04	Green Bay Trail	¤	16 mi., paved/screenings
	North Shore Path	¤	16 mi., screenings
	Evanston Paths	¤	7 mi., paved
	Illinois Beach State Park	¤	8 mi., screenings
	Zion Path	¤	4 mi., paved
IL05	Chicago Lakefront	¤	20 mi., paved
IL06	North Branch	¤	20 mi., paved
	Nearby Community Bikeways	¤	streets
IL07	Northwest Cook County		
	Arlington Hgts. Bikeways	¤	7 mi., streets
	Busse Woods FP	¤	11 mi., paved
	Deer Grove FP	¤¤	4 mi., paved
	Palatine Trails & Bikeways	¤	15 mi., paved/streets
IL08	South Cook County		
	Arie Crown FP	¤	3 mi., paved
	Salt Creek FP	¤	7 mi., paved
	Thorn Creek FP	¤	8 mi., paved
	Tinley Creek FP	¤	13 mi., paved
IL09	Palos FP (Cook Cnty)	¤	40 mi, groomed, woods, prairie
	Waterfall Glen FP (DuPage)	¤	9 mi, screenings
IL10	I&M Canal Bicycle Trail	¤	56 mi, screenings
IL11	McHenry & Boone County Trails		
	Long Prairie Trail	¤	8 mi, paved
	Moraine Hills State Park	¤	9 mi, screenings, small hills, woods
	Prairie Path - North Segment	¤	8 mi, crushed stone, dirt, railbed
	Prairie Path - South Segment	¤	5 mi, screenings
IL12	Des Plaines River Trail	¤	49 mi, screenings
	Greenbelt FP	¤	4 mi, screenings
	Grant Woods FP	¤	3 mi, screenings

| ¤ | **Mountain Biking Trails** | ¤ | **Leisure Biking Trails** |

Map#	Illinois		Basic Data
IL13	Peoria Area Trails		
	Rock Island State Trail	¤	28 mi, screenings
	Pimiteoui Trail/Bikeway	¤	13 mi, paved trails & streets
	River Trail of Illinois	¤	11 mi, paved/screenings
IL14	DuPage County Forest Preserves		
	Blackwell FP	¤	3 mi, screenings
	Churchill Woods FP	¤	2 mi, screenings, natural
	Danada FP	¤	2 mi, screenings
	Fullersburg Woods FP	¤	2 mi, paved, screenings
	Green Valley FP	¤	6 mi, groomed, woods, prairie
	Herrick's Grove FP	¤	4 mi, screenings
	McDowell Grove FP	¤	6 mi, groomed, woods, prairie
	Pratt's Wayne Woods FP	¤	7 mi, groomed, woods, prairie

Map#	Iowa		Basic Data
IA01	Northwest Iowa Trails		
	Great River Road Trail	¤	16 mi, designated shoulder
	Heritage Trail	¤	26 mi, screenings
	Prairie Farmer Rec. Trail	¤	17 mi, screenings
IA02	Cedar Valley Nature Trail	¤	52 mi, screenings
	Sax & Fox Trail	¤	8 mi, screenings
IA03	Waterloo & Cedar Falls Trails	¤	31 mi, paved
	Comet Trail	¤	6 mi, screenings/natural
	Pioneer Trail	¤	12 mi, screenings/natural
	Shell Rock River Trail	¤	5 mi, paved/ballast
IA05	Des Moines Area Trails - East		
	Chichaqua Valley Trail	¤	20 mi, screenings
	East River Bike Trail	¤	6 mi, paved
	Heart of Iowa Nature Trail	¤¤	32 mi, paved/ballast
IA06	Des Moines Area Trails - West		
	Bill Riley Bike Trail	¤	2 mi, paved
	Clive Greenbelt Trail	¤	6 mi, paved/screenings
	Great Western Trail	¤	17 mi, paved/screenings
	Saylorville-Des Moines Riv Tr	¤	24 mi, paved
IA07	Raccoon River Valley Trail	¤	34 mi, paved
	Sauk Rail Trail	¤	33 mi, paved/ballast
IA08	Wabash Trace Nature Trail	¤¤	63 mi, screenings/ballast, old railbed
	Cinder Path	¤	14 mi, cinder

¤ **Mountain Biking Trails**   ¤ **Leisure Biking Trails**

113

Detail Trail Maps Available (Continued)

Map#	Michigan		Basic Data
MI01	Hart-Montague Trail	¤	23 mi., paved
	Kal-Haven State Trail	¤	34 mi., screenings
MI02	Southwest - Metro Area Trails		
	Battle Creek-Linear Park	¤	17 mi, paved
	Grand Rapids-Kent Trail Trail	¤	13 mi, paved
	Lansing-River Trail	¤	6 mi, paved
MI03	Detroit Area Trails		
	I-275 Bike Path	¤	45 mi, paved
	Maybury State Park	¤	4 mi, paved
	Paint Creek Trail	¤	11 mi, crushed stone
	West Bloomfield Tr Network	¤	4 mi, ballast
MI04	Detroit Area-Metro Park Trails		
	Hudson Mills	¤	3 mi, paved
	Indian Springs	¤	8 mi, paved
	Kensington	¤	8 mi, paved
	Lower Huron	¤	4 mi, paved
	Oakwoods	¤	3 mi, paved
	Stoney Creek	¤	6 mi, paved
	Willow	¤	5 mi, paved
MI20	Southwest - Mountain Biking		
	Baw Beese Trail	¤¤¤	6 mi, stone, ballast, natural
	Fort Custer Recreational Area	¤	7 mi, woods, small hills
	Hofma Reserve	¤	4 mi, woods, open areas
	Ionia Recreation Area	¤	5 mi, wetlands, meadows, woods
	Yankee Springs	¤	12 mi, bogs, marshes, rugged
MI25	Northwest-UP-Mountain Biking		
	Bergland to Signaw Trail	¤	44 mi, ballast, sand, dirt, raidbed
	Iron Country Recreation Trail	¤	12 mi, ballast, sand, railbed
	Little Falls Trail	¤	7 mi, gravel, sand, dirt, railbed
	Stager-Crystal Falls Trail	¤	9 mi, ballast, sand, railbed
	State Line Trail	¤	89 mi, ballast, sand, railbed
	Watersmeet/Land O'Lakes Tr	¤	9 mi, ballast, sand, dirt, railbed

¤   **Mountain Biking Trails**   ¤   **Leisure Biking Trails**

Waterproof, Tear resistent, 2 color, 2 sides, 11 by 17 inches

Map#	Minnesota		Basic Data
MN01	Cannon Valley Trail	¤	20 mi, paved
	Root River State Trail	¤	35 mi, paved, natural
MN02	Hennepin Parks Trails		
	Baker Park Reserve	¤	6 mi, paved
	Carver Park Reserve	¤	9 mi, paved
	Cleary Lake Regional Park	¤	4 mi, paved
	Elm Creek Park Reserve	¤	9 mi, paved
	Hennepin Trail Corridor	¤	8 mi, paved
	Hyland Lake Park Reserve	¤	6 mi, paved
MN03	Heartland State Trail	¤	50 mi, paved/natural
	Itasca State Park	¤	17 mi, paved/natural
	Paul Bunyan State Trail	¤	
MN04	Luce Line Trail	¤¤	64 mi, screenings/natural
MN05	Minneapolis/St. Paul Trails	¤	63 mi, paved/shoulders/streets
	Gateway Trail	¤	20 mi, paved
MN06	Rochester (City) Trails	¤	100+ mi, paved/shoulders/streets
	Douglas State Trail	¤	13 mi, paved
	Whitewater Wildlife MA	¤	natural, ungroomed
MN07	Sakatak Singing Hills Trail	¤	39 mi, paved/screenings
	River Bend Nature Trail	¤	10 mi, screenings/natural
MN08	Willard Munger State Trail	¤	51 mi, paved
	Saint Croix State Park	¤	6 mi, paved
	Western Waterfront Trail	¤	5 mi, screenings
MN20	South East - Mountain Biking		
	Bronk Unit (R. Doyer SF)	¤	7 mi, dirt, woods, ridges
	Snake Creek (R. Doyer SF)	¤	9 mi, dirt, rocky, forest,slopes
	Trout Valley (R. Doyer SF)	¤	8.5 mi, dirt, rocky , forest, riv. vall.
	Myre Big Island State Park	¤	7 mi, grass, hills, lakes

¤ **Mountain Biking Trails**   ¤ **Leisure Biking Trails**

Detail Trail Maps Available (Continued)

Map#	Minnesota (Continued)		Basic Data
MN21	Minn./St. Paul area - Mtn. Biking		
	Elm Creek Park Reserve	¤	5 mi, grass, woods
	Lebanon Hill	¤	3 mi, grass, dirt, woods, hills
	Minnesota River Valley State Pk.		
	Louisville Swamp	¤	20 mi, grass, dirt, lowlands
	Lawrence Unit	¤	14 mi, woods, wetlands, prairie
	Mound Springs Park	¤	3 mi, grass, dirt, woods, lowlands
	Murphy-Hanrehand Park	¤	6 mi, grass, steep hills, lowlands
MN22	East Central - Mountain Biking		
	Jay Cooke State Park	¤	12 mi, grass, rocks, forest, steep
	Saint Croix State Park	¤	13 mi, forest, meadows, marshes
	Saint Croix State Forest	¤	18 mi, woods, rock, hills, flat
	Savanna Portage State Park	¤	12 mi, dirt roads, hills, bogs
MN23	North Central - Mountain Biking		
	Lake Bemidji State Park	¤	9 mi, woods, hills, swamps
	Paul Bunyan State Park	¤	10 mi, forest, roads, bogs, marsh
	Pillsbury State Forest	¤	11 mi, forest, ponds, hills
	Sugar Hills Trail	¤	12 mi, logging rds, hills ridges
	Washburn Lake Trail	¤	13 mi, forest, rolling hills
MN24	North East - Mountain Biking		
	Gegoka/Flathorn	¤	45 mi, roads, woods, wetlands
	Gooseberry Falls State Park	¤	2 mi, forest, shoreline
	Pincushion Mountain	¤	6 mi, forest, lowlands, bluffs
	Split Rock State Park	¤	8 mi, woods, flat to steep hills
	Whitefish Lake	¤	20 mi, woods, hills, marshes
MN25	North East - Mountain Biking		
	Big Aspen Trail	¤	9 mi, forest, logging roads
	Giants Ridge - Laurentain Tr	¤	6 mi, moderate hills, gravel, grass
	Giants Ridge - Silver Trail	¤	6 mi, woods, lakes, hills
	Giants Ridge - Wayne Lake	¤	10 mi, woods, ridges, lake, rocks
	McCarthy Beach State Park	¤	15 mi, woods, hills, valleys, lake
	Scenic State Park	¤	5 mi, woods, hills, flat areas

¤   **Mountain Biking Trails**   ¤   **Leisure Biking Trails**

Waterproof, Tear resistent, 2 color, 2 sides, 11 by 17 inches

Map#	Wisconsin		Basic Data
WI01	Elroy-Sparta State Trail	¤	32 mi, screenings
	Wildcat Mountain State Park	¤	park roads
WI02	LaCrosse River Trail	¤	22 mi, screenings
WI03	Great River State Trail	¤	23 mi, screenings
	Perrot State Park	¤	9 mi, prairie, bluffs, woods
WI04	Military Ridge State Park	¤	40 mi, screenings
	Governor Dodge St Pk	¤	9 mi, forests, meadows
WI05	Cheese Country Rec Trail	¤¤	47 mi, ballast, old railbed,
	Pecatonica Trail	¤	17 mi, crushed stone
WI06	Sugar River State Park	¤	24 mi, screenings
WI07	'400' Bike Trail	¤	22 mi, screenings
	Omaha Trail	¤	13 mi, paved
WI08	Buffalo River State Park Trail	¤	36 mi, ballast, old railbed
	Chippewa River Trail	¤	13 mi, screenings
	Red Cedar Bicycle Trail	¤	15 mi, screenings
WI09	Wild Goose State Trail	¤	35 mi, screenings
WI10	Waukesha County Trails		
	Bugline Recreation Trail	¤	12 mi, screenings
	New Berlin State Trail	¤	6 mi, screenings
	Lapham Peak	¤	4 mi, woods, hills, grass
	Waukesha bikeways	¤	streets
WI11	Racine & Kenosha Counties		
	Kenosha County	¤	14 mi, screenings/streets
	North Shore Trail - Racine	¤	3 mi, screenings
	M.R.K. Trail - Racine	¤	5 mi, screenings
	Burlington Trail - Racine	¤	4 mi, screenings
	Waterford-Wind Trail - Racine	¤	5 mi, screenings
	Bikeways - Racine	¤	100+ mi, roads
WI12	Milwaukee County Trails	¤	90 mi, paved/streets
WI13	Madison (city) & Dane County	¤	100+mi, paved/streets
WI14	Door County Bikeways	¤	100+mi, back roads
	Door County State Parks	¤	29 mi, forest, marsh, meadows
	Ahnapee State Trail	¤	15 mi, screenings, ballast

¤ **Mountain Biking Trails**   ¤ **Leisure Biking Trails**

Detail Trail Maps Available (Continued)

Map#	Wisconsin (Continued)		Basic Data
WI16	Glacial Drumlin State Trail	¤	47 mi, screenings
WI17	Kettle Moraine S.F. (N&S)	¤	woods, grass, hills
WI20	Tuscobia-Park Falls Trail	¤	76 mi, ballast, old railbed
	Flambeau River State Forest	¤	100+mi, forest, steep hills
WI21	Bearskin State Trail	¤	18 mi, screenings
	Alternate Mtn Biking Trails	¤	19 mi, woods, grass, hills
	Alternate Back Rd Bikeways	¤	100+ mi, backroads
WI22	Old Plank Road Trail	¤	23 mi, paved/natural
	Outagame-Winnebago Trail	¤	20 mi, screenings
	Fox Cities Bikeways	¤	39 mi, roads
WI31	South East - Mountain Biking		
	Bong State Recreation Trail	¤	4 mi, grass, woods
	Devil's Lake State Park	¤	7 mi, grassy
	Harrington Beach State Park	¤	2 mi, grass, sand, lake shore
	Kohlar-Andrae State Park	¤	3 mi, grassy
	Lapham Peak	¤	mi, hills, woods, grass
WI32	South West - Mountain Biking		
	Blue Mound State Park	¤	4 mi, grass, woods, hills
	Governor Dodge State Park	¤	9 mi, forests, meadows
	Mirror Lake State Park	¤	9.2 mi., woods, gravel, sand
	Wildcat Mtn. State Park	¤	Roads
	Wyalusing State Park	¤	12 mi, woods, hills, grass
WI33	North East - Mountain Biking		
	Door Cnty - Newport Bch SP	¤	12 mi, forest, wetlands, meadows
	Door Cnty - Peninsula SP	¤	13 mi, forests, marsh, meadows
	Door Cnty - Potawatomi SP	¤	4 mi, flat to rolling & steep
	High Cliff	¤	8 mi, woods, Indian Mounds
	Oconto County Rec Trail	¤	30 mi, forest, farmland, grass
	Point Beach State Park	¤	4 mi, woods, beach, grass

¤ **Mountain Biking Trails**   ¤ **Leisure Biking Trails**

Waterproof, Tear resistent, 2 color, 2 sides, 11 by 17 inches

Map#	Wisconsin (Continued)		Basic Data
WI34	West Central - Mountain Biking		
	Black River SF - Castle Mnd	¤	5 mi, woods, hills, level
	Black River SF - Pigeon Ck	¤	4 mi, woods, level, grass, dirt
	Black River SF - Smerekar Tr	¤	8 mi, woods, steep hills
	Black River SF - Wildcat Trail	¤	7 mi, grass, hills heavy woods
	Lake Wissota	¤	11 mi, grass, woods
	Lowes Creek County Park	¤	5 mi, woods, prairie, hills
WI35	North Central - Mountain Biking		
	Council Grounds State Park	¤	3 mi, woods, hills, grass
	Hiawatha Trail	¤	7 mi, ballast, old railbed
	Lumberjack Trail	¤	12 mi, woods, rolling, grass, dirt
	Madeline Lake Trail	¤	10 mi, grassy, hills
	McNaughton Lake Trail	¤	12 mi, grass, rolling hills
	Nine Mile State Forest Trail	¤	25 mi, woods, uplands, marshes
	Shannon Lake Trail	¤	8 mi, woods, gently rolling
WI36	Pine Line Recreation Trail	¤	26 mi, screenings
	Jaycee Trail	¤	15 mi, groomed
	Timms Hill Trail	¤	10 mi, groomed
WI37	North West - Mountain Biking		
	Black Lake Trail	¤	4 mi, woods, lake
	Brule River State Forest	¤	6 mi, rolling hills, deep forests
	Copper Falls State Park	¤	8 mi, level to steep hills, rocks
	Governor Knowles SF	¤	not posted, rolling hills, valleys
	Rock Lake Trail	¤	25 mi, woods, hills ridges
	Wintergreen Ski/Hiking Area	¤	15 mi, forests, ridges, marshes

¤	**Mountain Biking Trails**	¤	**Leisure Biking Trails**

Map# State - Trail Reference Maps

	IL90	Illinois
	IA90	Iowa
	MI90	Michigan
	MN90	Minnesota
	WI90	Wisconsin

Trail Index

	Area	Page
Black Lake Trail	NW	78
Black River State Forest	WC	50
Blue Mound State Park	SW	26
Bong State Recreation Trail	SE	08
Brule River State Forest	NW	80
Cable Cluster - CAMBA	NW	98
Castle Mound Park	WC	52
Chequamegon Nat'l. For. *Taylor County*	NC	73
Copper Falls State Park	NW	82
Council Grounds State Park	NC	62
Delta Cluster - CAMBA	NW	94
Devil's Lake State Park	SE	10
Door County Overview	NE	41
Drummond Cluster - CAMBA	NW	96
Flambeau River State Forest	NW	84
Governor Dodge State Park	SW	28
Governor Knowles State Forest	NW	79
Harrington Beach State Park	SE	12
Hayward Cluster- CAMBA	NW	102
Hiawatha Trail	NC	64
High Cliff State Park	NE	36
Jaycee Trail	NC	73
Kettle Moraine St. Forest - North Unit	SE	14
Kettle Moraine St. Forest - South Unit	SE	18
Kohler-Andrae State Park	SE	13

	Area	Page
Lake Wissota State Park	WC	56
Lapham Peak	SE	23
Lowes Creek County Park	WC	58
Lumberjack Trail	NC	66
Madeline Lake Trails	NC	68
McNaughton Lake Trails	NC	69
Mirror Lake State Park	SW	30
Namakagon Cluster- CAMBA	NW	104
Newport State Park	NE	40
Nine Mile County Forest Trail	NC	70
Oconto County Recreational Trail	NE	38
Peninsula State Park	NE	42
Perrot State Park	SW	31
Pigeon Creek	WC	53
Point Beach State Forest	NE	46
Potawatomi State Park	NE	44
Rock Lake	NW	88
Seeley Cluster - CAMBA	NW	100
Shannon Lake Trail	NC	72
Smrekar Trail	WC	54
Timm's Hill Trail	NC	73
Tuscobia-Park Falls State Trail	NW	86
Wildcat Mountain State Park	SW	27
Wildcat Trail	WC	54
Wintergreen	NW	89
Wyalusing State Park	SW	32

Notes

Order Form
American Bike Trails
1430 Miner Street, Suite 525
Des Plaines, IL 60016

Name_____

Address _____

City, State, Zip _____

Phone (   ) _____ *In case of a question*

Method of Payment

☐ Check   ☐ Mastercard   ☐ Visa

Card Number _____

Expire Date_____ Signature _____

Qty.	Map No.	Description	Price Ea.	Total

	COST		
Trail Maps .... **$4.95** (STATE CODE FOLLOWED BY 01-50)	**Merchandise Total**		
State Trail **Reference Maps**..... **$2.95** (STATE CODE FOLLOWED BY #90)	**Shipping & Handling**	$3.00
	IL residents add 6.5% sales tax	
Add'l copies **of this book** **$14.95**	**TOTAL AMOUNT**	

Notes